The Devil's Disciple

By George Bernard Shaw

A Digireads.com Book
Digireads.com Publishing
16212 Riggs Rd
Stilwell, KS, 66085

The Devil's Disciple
By George Bernard Shaw
ISBN: 1-4209-2894-5

Please visit *www.digireads.com*

ACT I

At the most wretched hour between a black night and a wintry morning in the year 1777, MRS. DUDGEON, of New Hampshire, is sitting up in the kitchen and general dwelling room of her farm house on the outskirts of the town of Websterbridge. She is not a prepossessing woman. No woman looks her best after sitting up all night; and MRS. DUDGEON's face, even at its best, is grimly trenched by the channels into which the barren forms and observances of a dead Puritanism can pen a bitter temper and a fierce pride. She is an elderly matron who has worked hard and got nothing by it except dominion and detestation in her sordid home, and an unquestioned reputation for piety and respectability among her neighbors, to whom drink and debauchery are still so much more tempting than religion and rectitude, that they conceive goodness simply as self-denial. This conception is easily extended to others—denial, and finally generalized as covering anything disagreeable. So MRS. DUDGEON, being exceedingly disagreeable, is held to be exceedingly good. Short of flat felony, she enjoys complete license except for amiable weaknesses of any sort, and is consequently, without knowing it, the most licentious woman in the parish on the strength of never having broken the seventh commandment or missed a Sunday at the Presbyterian church.

The year 1777 is the one in which the passions roused of the breaking off of the American colonies from England, more by their own weight than their own will, boiled up to shooting point, the shooting being idealized to the English mind as suppression of rebellion and maintenance of British dominion, and to the American as defence of liberty, resistance to tyranny, and self-sacrifice on the altar of the Rights of Man. Into the merits of these idealizations it is not here necessary to inquire: suffice it to say, without prejudice, that they have convinced both Americans and English that the most high minded course for them to pursue is to kill as many of one another as possible, and that military operations to that end are in full swing, morally supported by confident requests from the clergy of both sides for the blessing of God on their arms.

Under such circumstances many other women besides this disagreeable MRS. DUDGEON find themselves sitting up all night waiting for news. Like her, too, they fall asleep towards morning at the risk of nodding themselves into the kitchen fire. MRS. DUDGEON sleeps with a shawl over her head, and her feet on a broad fender of iron laths, the step of the domestic altar of the fireplace, with its huge hobs and boiler, and its hinged arm above the smoky mantel-shelf for roasting. The plain kitchen table is opposite the fire, at her elbow, with a candle on it in a tin sconce. Her chair, like all the others in the room, is uncushioned and unpainted; but as it has a round railed back and a seat conventionally moulded to the sitter's curves, it is comparatively a chair of state. The room has three doors, one on the same side as the fireplace, near the corner, leading to the best bedroom; one, at the opposite end of the opposite wall, leading to the scullery and washhouse; and the house door, with its latch, heavy lock, and clumsy wooden bar, in the front wall, between the window in its middle and the corner next the bedroom door. Between the door and the window a rack of pegs suggests to the deductive observer that the men of the house are all away, as there are no hats or coats on them. On the other side of the window the clock hangs on a nail, with its white wooden dial, black iron weights, and brass pendulum. Between the clock and the corner, a big cupboard, locked, stands on a dwarf dresser full of common crockery.

On the side opposite the fireplace, between the door and the corner, a shamelessly ugly black horsehair sofa stands against the wall. An inspection of its stridulous surface shows that MRS. DUDGEON is not alone. A girl of sixteen or seventeen has fallen asleep on it. She is a wild, timid looking creature with black hair and tanned skin. Her frock, a scanty garment, is rent, weatherstained, berrystained, and by no means scrupulously clean. It hangs on her with a freedom which, taken with her brown legs and bare feet, suggests no great stock of underclothing.

Suddenly there comes a tapping at the door, not loud enough to wake the sleepers. Then knocking, which disturbs MRS. DUDGEON a little. Finally the latch is tried, whereupon she springs up at once.

MRS. DUDGEON. [*threateningly*]. Well, why don't you open the door? [*She sees that the girl is asleep and immediately raises a clamor of heartfelt vexation.*] Well, dear, dear me! Now this is—[*shaking her*] wake up, wake up: do you hear?

THE GIRL. [*sitting up*]. What is it?

MRS. DUDGEON. Wake up; and be ashamed of yourself, you unfeeling sinful girl, falling asleep like that, and your father hardly cold in his grave.

THE GIRL. [*half asleep still*]. I didn't mean to. I dropped off—

MRS. DUDGEON. [*cutting her short*]. Oh yes, you've plenty of excuses, I daresay. Dropped off! [*Fiercely, as the knocking recommences.*] Why don't you get up and let your uncle in? after me waiting up all night for him! [*She pushes her rudely off the sofa.*] There: I'll open the door: much good you are to wait up. Go and mend that fire a bit.

The girl, cowed and wretched, goes to the fire and puts a log on. MRS. DUDGEON unbars the door and opens it, letting into the stuffy kitchen a little of the freshness and a great deal of the chill of the dawn, also her second son CHRISTY, a fattish, stupid, fair-haired, round-faced man of about 22, muffled in a plaid shawl and grey overcoat. He hurries, shivering, to the fire, leaving MRS. DUDGEON to shut the door.

CHRISTY. [*at the fire*]. F—f—f! but it is cold. [*Seeing the girl, and staring lumpishly at her.*] Why, who are you?

THE GIRL. [*shyly*]. Essie.

MRS. DUDGEON. Oh you may well ask. [*To ESSIE.*] Go to your room, child, and lie down since you haven't feeling enough to keep you awake. Your history isn't fit for your own ears to hear.

ESSIE. I—

MRS. DUDGEON. [*peremptorily*]. Don't answer me, Miss; but show your obedience by doing what I tell you. [*ESSIE, almost in tears, crosses the room to the door near the sofa.*] And don't forget your prayers. [*ESSIE goes out.*] She'd have gone to bed last night just as if nothing had happened if I'd let her.

CHRISTY. [*phlegmatically*]. Well, she can't be expected to feel Uncle Peter's death like one of the family.

MRS. DUDGEON. What are you talking about, child? Isn't she his daughter—the punishment of his wickedness and shame? [*She assaults her chair by sitting down.*]

CHRISTY. [*staring*]. Uncle Peter's daughter!

MRS. DUDGEON. Why else should she be here? D'ye think I've not had enough trouble and care put upon me bringing up my own girls, let alone you and your good-for-nothing brother, without having your uncle's bastards—

CHRISTY. [*interrupting her with an apprehensive glance at the door by which ESSIE went out*]. Sh! She may hear you.

MRS. DUDGEON. [*raising her voice*]. Let her hear me. People who fear God don't fear to give the devil's work its right name. [*CHRISTY, soullessly indifferent to the strife of Good and Evil, stares at the fire, warming himself.*] Well, how long are you going to stare there like a stuck pig? What news have you for me?

CHRISTY. [*taking off his hat and shawl and going to the rack to hang them up*]. The minister is to break the news to you. He'll be here presently.

MRS. DUDGEON. Break what news?

CHRISTY. [*standing on tiptoe, from boyish habit, to hang his hat up, though he is quite tall enough to reach the peg, and speaking with callous placidity, considering the nature of the announcement*]. Father's dead too.

MRS. DUDGEON. [*stupent*]. Your father!

CHRISTY. [*sulkily, coming back to the fire and warming himself again, attending much more to the fire than to his mother*]. Well, it's not my fault. When we got to Nevinstown we found him ill in bed. He didn't know us at first. The minister sat up with him and sent me away. He died in the night.

MRS. DUDGEON. [*bursting into dry angry tears*]. Well, I do think this is hard on me—very hard on me. His brother, that was a disgrace to us all his life, gets hanged on the public gallows as a rebel; and your father, instead of staying at home where his duty was, with his own family, goes after him and dies, leaving everything on my shoulders. After sending this girl to me to take care of, too! [*She plucks her shawl vexedly over her ears.*] It's sinful, so it is; downright sinful.

CHRISTY. [*with a slow, bovine cheerfulness, after a pause*]. I think it's going to be a fine morning, after all.

MRS. DUDGEON. [*railing at him*]. A fine morning! And your father newly dead! Where's your feelings, child?

CHRISTY. [*obstinately*]. Well, I didn't mean any harm. I suppose a man may make a remark about the weather even if his father's dead.

MRS. DUDGEON. [*bitterly*]. A nice comfort my children are to me! One son a fool, and the other a lost sinner that's left his home to live with smugglers and gypsies and villains, the scum of the earth!

Someone knocks.

CHRISTY. [*without moving*]. That's the minister.

MRS. DUDGEON. [*sharply*]. Well, aren't you going to let Mr. Anderson in?

CHRISTY goes sheepishly to the door. MRS. DUDGEON buries her face in her hands, as it is her duty as a widow to be overcome with grief. CHRISTY opens the door, and admits the minister, ANTHONY ANDERSON, a shrewd, genial, ready Presbyterian divine of about 50, with something of the authority of his profession in his bearing.

But it is an altogether secular authority, sweetened by a conciliatory, sensible manner not at all suggestive of a quite thoroughgoing other-worldliness. He is a strong, healthy man, too, with a thick, sanguine neck; and his keen, cheerful mouth cuts into somewhat fleshy corners. No doubt an excellent parson, but still a man capable of making the most of this world, and perhaps a little apologetically conscious of getting on better with it than a sound Presbyterian ought.

ANDERSON. [*to CHRISTY, at the door, looking at MRS. DUDGEON whilst he takes off his cloak*]. Have you told her?

CHRISTY. She made me. [*He shuts the door; yawns; and loafs across to the sofa where he sits down and presently drops off to sleep.*]

ANDERSON looks compassionately at MRS. DUDGEON. Then he hangs his cloak and hat on the rack. MRS. DUDGEON dries her eyes and looks up at him.

ANDERSON. Sister: the Lord has laid his hand very heavily upon you.

MRS. DUDGEON. [with intensely recalcitrant resignation]. It's His will, I suppose; and I must bow to it. But I do think it hard. What call had Timothy to go to Springtown, and remind everybody that he belonged to a man that was being hanged?—and [*spitefully*] that deserved it, if ever a man did.

ANDERSON. [*gently*]. They were brothers, Mrs. Dudgeon.

MRS. DUDGEON. Timothy never acknowledged him as his brother after we were married: he had too much respect for me to insult me with such a brother. Would such a selfish wretch as Peter have come thirty miles to see Timothy hanged, do you think? Not thirty yards, not he. However, I must bear my cross as best I may: least said is soonest mended.

ANDERSON. [very grave, coming down to the fire to stand with his back to it]. Your eldest son was present at the execution, Mrs. Dudgeon.

MRS. DUDGEON. [*disagreeably surprised*]. Richard?

ANDERSON. [*nodding*]. Yes.

MRS. DUDGEON. [*vindictively*]. Let it be a warning to him. He may end that way himself, the wicked, dissolute, godless— [*she suddenly stops; her voice fails; and she asks, with evident dread*] Did Timothy see him?

ANDERSON. Yes.

MRS. DUDGEON. [*holding her breath*]. Well?

ANDERSON. He only saw him in the crowd: they did not speak. [*MRS. DUDGEON, greatly relieved, exhales the pent up breath and sits at her ease again.*] Your husband was greatly touched and impressed by his brother's awful death. [*MRS. DUDGEON sneers. ANDERSON breaks off to demand with some indignation*] Well, wasn't it only natural, Mrs. Dudgeon? He softened towards his prodigal son in that moment. He sent for him to come to see him.

MRS. DUDGEON. [*her alarm renewed*]. Sent for Richard!

ANDERSON. Yes; but Richard would not come. He sent his father a message; but I'm sorry to say it was a wicked message—an awful message.

MRS. DUDGEON. What was it?

ANDERSON. That he would stand by his wicked uncle, and stand against his good parents, in this world and the next.

MRS. DUDGEON. [*implacably*]. He will be punished for it. He will be punished for it—in both worlds.

ANDERSON. That is not in our hands, Mrs. Dudgeon.

MRS. DUDGEON. Did I say it was, Mr. Anderson. We are told that the wicked shall be punished. Why should we do our duty and keep God's law if there is to be no difference made between us and those who follow their own likings and dislikings, and make a jest of us and of their Maker's word?

ANDERSON. Well, Richard's earthly father has been merciful and his heavenly judge is the father of us all.

MRS. DUDGEON. [*forgetting herself*]. Richard's earthly father was a softheaded—

ANDERSON. [*shocked*]. Oh!

MRS. DUDGEON. [*with a touch of shame*]. Well, I am Richard's mother. If I am against him who has any right to be for him? [*Trying to conciliate him.*] Won't you sit down, Mr.

Anderson? I should have asked you before; but I'm so troubled.

ANDERSON. Thank you—[*He takes a chair from beside the fireplace, and turns it so that he can sit comfortably at the fire. When he is seated he adds, in the tone of a man who knows that he is opening a difficult subject.*] Has Christy told you about the new will?

MRS. DUDGEON. [*all her fears returning*]. The new will! Did Timothy—? [*She breaks off, gasping, unable to complete the question.*]

ANDERSON. Yes. In his last hours he changed his mind.

MRS. DUDGEON. [*white with intense rage*]. And you let him rob me?

ANDERSON. I had no power to prevent him giving what was his to his own son.

MRS. DUDGEON. He had nothing of his own. His money was the money I brought him as my marriage portion. It was for me to deal with my own money and my own son. He dare not have done it if I had been with him; and well he knew it. That was why he stole away like a thief to take advantage of the law to rob me by making a new will behind my back. The more shame on you, Mr. Anderson,—you, a minister of the gospel—to act as his accomplice in such a crime.

ANDERSON. [*rising*]. I will take no offence at what you say in the first bitterness of your grief.

MRS. DUDGEON. [*contemptuously*]. Grief!

ANDERSON. Well, of your disappointment, if you can find it in your heart to think that the better word.

MRS. DUDGEON. My heart! My heart! And since when, pray, have you begun to hold up our hearts as trustworthy guides for us?

ANDERSON. [*rather guiltily*]. I—er—

MRS. DUDGEON. [*vehemently*]. Don't lie, Mr. Anderson. We are told that the heart of man is deceitful above all things, and desperately wicked. My heart belonged, not to Timothy, but to that poor wretched brother of his that has just ended his days with a rope round his neck—aye, to Peter Dudgeon. You know it: old Eli Hawkins, the man to whose pulpit you succeeded, though you are not worthy to loose his shoe latchet, told it you when he gave over our souls into your charge. He warned me and strengthened me against my heart, and made me marry a God-fearing man—as he thought. What else but that discipline has made me the woman I am? And you, you who followed your heart in your marriage, you talk to me of what I find in my heart. Go home to your pretty wife, man; and leave me to my prayers. [*She turns from him and leans with her elbows on the table, brooding over her wrongs and taking no further notice of him.*]

ANDERSON. [*willing enough to escape*]. The Lord forbid that I should come between you and the source of all comfort! [*He goes to the rack for his coat and hat.*]

MRS. DUDGEON. [*without looking at him*]. The Lord will know what to forbid and what to allow without your help.

ANDERSON. And whom to forgive, I hope—Eli Hawkins and myself, if we have ever set up our preaching against His law. [*He fastens his cloak, and is now ready to go.*] Just one word—on necessary business, Mrs. Dudgeon. There is the reading of the will to be gone through; and Richard has a right to be present. He is in the town; but he has the grace to say that he does not want to force himself in here.

MRS. DUDGEON. He shall come here. Does he expect us to leave his father's house for his convenience? Let them all come, and come quickly, and go quickly. They shall not make the will an excuse to shirk half their day's work. I shall be ready, never fear.

ANDERSON. [*coming back a step or two*]. Mrs. Dudgeon: I used to have some little influence with you. When did I lose it?

MRS. DUDGEON. [*still without turning to him*]. When you married for love. Now you're answered.

ANDERSON. Yes: I am answered. [*He goes out, musing.*]

MRS. DUDGEON. [*to herself, thinking of her husband*]. Thief! Thief!! [*She shakes herself angrily out of the chair; throws back the shawl from her head; and sets to work to prepare the room for the reading of the will, beginning by replacing*

ANDERSON's chair against the wall, and pushing back her own to the window. Then she calls, in her hard, driving, wrathful way] Christy. [*No answer: he is fast asleep.*] Christy. [*She shakes him roughly.*] Get up out of that; and be ashamed of yourself—sleeping, and your father dead! [*She returns to the table; puts the candle on the mantelshelf; and takes from the table drawer a red table cloth which she spreads.*]

CHRISTY. [*rising reluctantly*]. Well, do you suppose we are never going to sleep until we are out of mourning?

MRS. DUDGEON. I want none of your sulks. Here: help me to set this table. [*They place the table in the middle of the room, with CHRISTY's end towards the fireplace and MRS. DUDGEON's towards the sofa. CHRISTY drops the table as soon as possible, and goes to the fire, leaving his mother to make the final adjustments of its position.*] We shall have the minister back here with the lawyer and all the family to read the will before you have done toasting yourself. Go and wake that girl; and then light the stove in the shed: you can't have your breakfast here. And mind you wash yourself, and make yourself fit to receive the company. [*She punctuates these orders by going to the cupboard; unlocking it; and producing a decanter of wine, which has no doubt stood there untouched since the last state occasion in the family, and some glasses, which she sets on the table. Also two green ware plates, on one of which she puts a barnbrack with a knife beside it. On the other she shakes some biscuits out of a tin, putting back one or two, and counting the rest.*] Now mind: there are ten biscuits there: let there be ten there when I come back after dressing myself. And keep your fingers off the raisins in that cake. And tell Essie the same. I suppose I can trust you to bring in the case of stuffed birds without breaking the glass? [*She replaces the tin in the cupboard, which she locks, pocketing the key carefully.*]

CHRISTY. [*lingering at the fire*]. You'd better put the inkstand instead, for the lawyer.

MRS. DUDGEON. That's no answer to make to me, sir. Go and do as you're told. [*CHRISTY turns sullenly to obey.*] Stop:

take down that shutter before you go, and let the daylight in: you can't expect me to do all the heavy work of the house with a great heavy lout like you idling about.

CHRISTY takes the window bar out of its damps, and puts it aside; then opens the shutter, showing the grey morning. MRS. DUDGEON takes the sconce from the mantelshelf; blows out the candle; extinguishes the snuff by pinching it with her fingers, first licking them for the purpose; and replaces the sconce on the shelf.

CHRISTY. [*looking through the window*]. Here's the minister's wife.

MRS. DUDGEON. [displeased]. What! Is she coming here?

CHRISTY. Yes.

MRS. DUDGEON. What does she want troubling me at this hour, before I'm properly dressed to receive people?

CHRISTY. You'd better ask her.

MRS. DUDGEON. [*threateningly*]. You'd better keep a civil tongue in your head. [He goes sulkily towards the door. She comes after him, plying him with instructions.] Tell that girl to come to me as soon as she's had her breakfast. And tell her to make herself fit to be seen before the people. [*CHRISTY goes out and slams the door in her face.*] Nice manners, that! [*Someone knocks at the house door: she turns and cries inhospitably.*] Come in. [*JUDITH ANDERSON, the minister's wife, comes in. JUDITH is more than twenty years younger than her husband, though she will never be as young as he in vitality. She is pretty and proper and ladylike, and has been admired and petted into an opinion of herself sufficiently favorable to give her a self-assurance which serves her instead of strength. She has a pretty taste in dress, and in her face the pretty lines of a sentimental character formed by dreams. Even her little self-complacency is pretty, like a child's vanity. Rather a pathetic creature to any sympathetic observer who knows how rough a place the world is. One feels, on the whole, that ANDERSON might have chosen worse, and that she, needing protection, could not have chosen better.*] Oh, it's you, is it, Mrs. Anderson?

JUDITH. [*very politely—almost patronizingly*]. Yes. Can I do anything for you, Mrs. Dudgeon? Can I help to get the place ready before they come to read the will?

MRS. DUDGEON. [*stiffly*]. Thank you, Mrs. Anderson, my house is always ready for anyone to come into.

MRS. ANDERSON [*with complacent amiability*]. Yes, indeed it is. Perhaps you had rather I did not intrude on you just now.

MRS. DUDGEON. Oh, one more or less will make no difference this morning, Mrs. Anderson. Now that you're here, you'd better stay. If you wouldn't mind shutting the door! [*JUDITH smiles, implying "How stupid of me" and shuts it with an exasperating air of doing something pretty and becoming.*] That's better. I must go and tidy myself a bit. I suppose you don't mind stopping here to receive anyone that comes until I'm ready.

JUDITH. [*graciously giving her leave*]. Oh yes, certainly. Leave them to me, Mrs. Dudgeon; and take your time. [She *hangs her cloak and bonnet on the rack.*]

MRS. DUDGEON. [*half sneering*]. I thought that would be more in your way than getting the house ready. [*ESSIE comes back.*] Oh, here you are! [*Severely*] Come here: let me see you. [*ESSIE timidly goes to her. MRS. DUDGEON takes her roughly by the arm and pulls her round to inspect the results of her attempt to clean and tidy herself—results which show little practice and less conviction.*] Mm! That's what you call doing your hair properly, I suppose. It's easy to see what you are, and how you were brought up. [*She throws her arms away, and goes on, peremptorily.*] Now you listen to me and do as you're told. You sit down there in the corner by the fire; and when the company comes don't dare to speak until you're spoken to. [*ESSIE creeps away to the fireplace.*] Your father's people had better see you and know you're there: they're as much bound to keep you from starvation as I am. At any rate they might help. But let me have no chattering and making free with them, as if you were their equal. Do you hear?

ESSIE. Yes.

MRS. DUDGEON. Well, then go and do as you're told.

[*ESSIE sits down miserably on the corner of the fender furthest from the door.*] Never mind her, Mrs. Anderson: you know who she is and what she is. If she gives you any trouble, just tell me; and I'll settle accounts with her. [*MRS. DUDGEON goes into the bedroom, shutting the door sharply behind her as if even it had to be made to do its duty with a ruthless hand.*]

JUDITH. [*patronizing ESSIE, and arranging the cake and wine on the table more becomingly*]. You must not mind if your aunt is strict with you. She is a very good woman, and desires your good too.

ESSIE. [*in listless misery*]. Yes.

JUDITH. [*annoyed with ESSIE for her failure to be consoled and edified, and to appreciate the kindly condescension of the remark*]. You are not going to be sullen, I hope, Essie.

ESSIE. No.

JUDITH. That's a good girl! [*She places a couple of chairs at the table with their backs to the window, with a pleasant sense of being a more thoughtful housekeeper than MRS. DUDGEON.*] Do you know any of your father's relatives?

ESSIE. No. They wouldn't have anything to do with him: they were too religious. Father used to talk about Dick Dudgeon; but I never saw him.

JUDITH. [*ostentatiously shocked*]. Dick Dudgeon! Essie: do you wish to be a really respectable and grateful girl, and to make a place for yourself here by steady good conduct?

ESSIE. [*very half-heartedly*]. Yes.

JUDITH. Then you must never mention the name of Richard Dudgeon—never even think about him. He is a bad man.

ESSIE. What has he done?

JUDITH. You must not ask questions about him, Essie. You are too young to know what it is to be a bad man. But he is a smuggler; and he lives with gypsies; and he has no love for his mother and his family; and he wrestles and plays games on Sunday instead of going to church. Never let him into your presence, if you can help it, Essie; and try to keep yourself and all womanhood unspotted by contact with such men.

ESSIE. Yes.

JUDITH. [*again displeased*]. I am afraid you say Yes and No without thinking very deeply.

ESSIE. Yes. At least I mean—

JUDITH. [severely]. What do you mean?

ESSIE. [*almost crying*]. Only—my father was a smuggler; and— [*Someone knocks.*]

JUDITH. They are beginning to come. Now remember your aunt's directions, Essie; and be a good girl. [*CHRISTY comes back with the stand of stuffed birds under a glass case, and an inkstand, which he places on the table.*] Good morning, Mr. Dudgeon. Will you open the door, please: the people have come.

CHRISTY. Good morning. [*He opens the house door.*]

The morning is now fairly bright and warm; and ANDERSON, who is the first to enter, has left his cloak at home. He is accompanied by LAWYER HAWKINS, a brisk, middleaged man in brown riding gaiters and yellow breeches, looking as much squire as solicitor. He and ANDERSON are allowed precedence as representing the learned professions. After them comes the family, headed by the senior UNCLE, WILLIAM DUDGEON, a large, shapeless man, bottle-nosed and evidently no ascetic at table. His clothes are not the clothes, nor his anxious wife the wife, of a prosperous man. The junior UNCLE, TITUS DUDGEON, is a wiry little terrier of a man, with an immense and visibly purse-proud wife, both free from the cares of the WILLIAM household.

HAWKINS at once goes briskly to the table and takes the chair nearest the sofa, CHRISTY having left the inkstand there. He puts his hat on the floor beside him, and produces the will. UNCLE WILLIAM comes to the fire and stands on the hearth warming his coat tails, leaving MRS. WILLIAM derelict near the door. UNCLE TITUS, who is the lady's man of the family, rescues her by giving her his disengaged arm and bringing her to the sofa, where he sits down warmly between his own lady and his brother's. Anderson hangs up his hat and waits for a word with JUDITH.

JUDITH. She will be here in a moment. Ask them to wait. [*She taps at the bedroom door. Receiving an answer from within, she opens it and passes through.*]

ANDERSON. [*taking his place at the table at the opposite end to HAWKINS*]. Our poor afflicted sister will be with us in a moment. Are we all here?

CHRISTY. [*at the house door, which he has just shut*]. All except Dick.

The callousness with which CHRISTY names the reprobate jars on the moral sense of the family. UNCLE WILLIAM shakes his head slowly and repeatedly. MRS. TITUS catches her breath convulsively through her nose. Her husband speaks.

UNCLE TITUS. Well, I hope he will have the grace not to come. I hope so.

THE DUDGEONS all murmur assent, except CHRISTY, who goes to the window and posts himself there, looking out. HAWKINS smiles secretively as if he knew something that would change their tune if they knew it. ANDERSON is uneasy: the love of solemn family councils, especially funereal ones, is not in his nature. JUDITH appears at the bedroom door.

JUDITH. [*with gentle impressiveness*]. Friends, Mrs. Dudgeon. [*She takes the chair from beside the fireplace; and places it for MRS. DUDGEON, who comes from the bedroom in black, with a clean handkerchief to her eyes. All rise, except ESSIE. Mrs. TITUS and Mrs. WILLIAM produce equally clean handkerchiefs and weep. It is an affecting moment.*]

UNCLE WILLIAM. Would it comfort you, sister, if we were to offer up a prayer?

UNCLE TITUS. Or sing a hymn?

ANDERSON. [*rather hastily*]. I have been with our sister this morning already, friends. In our hearts we ask a blessing.

ALL. [*except ESSIE*]. Amen.

They all sit down, except JUDITH, who stands behind MRS. DUDGEON's chair.

JUDITH. [*to ESSIE*]. Essie: did you say Amen?

ESSIE. [*scaredly*]. No.

JUDITH. Then say it, like a good girl.

ESSIE. Amen.

UNCLE WILLIAM. [*encouragingly*]. That's right: that's right. We know who you are; but we are willing to be kind to you if you are a good girl and deserve it. We are all equal before the Throne.

This republican sentiment does not please the women, who are convinced that the Throne is precisely the place where their superiority, often questioned in this world, will be recognized and rewarded.

CHRISTY. [*at the window*]. Here's Dick.

ANDERSON and HAWKINS look round sociably. Essie, with a gleam of interest breaking through her misery, looks up. CHRISTY grins and gapes expectantly at the door. The rest are petrified with the intensity of their sense of Virtue menaced with outrage by the approach of flaunting Vice. The reprobate appears in the doorway, graced beyond his alleged merits by the morning sunlight. He is certainly the best looking member of the family; but his expression is reckless and sardonic, his manner defiant and satirical, his dress picturesquely careless. Only his forehead and mouth betray an extraordinary steadfastness, and his eyes are the eyes of a fanatic.

RICHARD. [*on the threshold, taking off his hat*]. Ladies and gentlemen: your servant, your very humble servant. [*With this comprehensive insult, he throws his hat to CHRISTY with a suddenness that makes him jump like a negligent wicket keeper, and comes into the middle of the room, where he turns and deliberately surveys the company.*] How happy you all look! how glad to see me! [*He turns towards MRS. DUDGEON's chair; and his lip rolls up horribly from his dog tooth as he meets her look of undisguised hatred.*] Well, mother: keeping up appearances as usual? that's right, that's right. [*JUDITH pointedly moves away from his neighborhood to the other side of the kitchen, holding her skirt instinctively as if to save it from contamination. UNCLE TITUS promptly marks his approval of her action by rising from the sofa, and placing a chair for her to sit down upon.]* What! Uncle William! I haven't seen you since you gave up drinking. [*Poor UNCLE WILLIAM, shamed, would protest; but RICHARD claps him heartily on his shoulder, adding*] you have given it up, haven't you? [*releasing him with a playful push*] of course you have: quite right too; you overdid it. [*He turns away from UNCLE WILLIAM and makes for the sofa.*] And now, where is that upright horsedealer Uncle Titus? Uncle Titus: come forth. [*He comes upon him holding the chair as JUDITH sits down.*] As usual, looking after the ladies.

UNCLE TITUS. [*indignantly*]. Be ashamed of yourself, sir—

RICHARD. [*interrupting him and shaking his hand in spite of him*]. I am: I am; but I am proud of my uncle—proud of all my relatives [*again surveying them*] who could look at them and not be proud and joyful? [*UNCLE TITUS, overborne, resumes his seat on the sofa. RICHARD turns to the table.*] Ah, Mr. Anderson, still at the good work, still shepherding them. Keep them up to the mark, minister, keep them up to the mark. Come! [*with a spring he seats himself on the table and takes up the decanter*] clink a glass with me, Pastor, for the sake of old times.

ANDERSON. You know, I think, Mr. Dudgeon, that I do not drink before dinner.

RICHARD. You will, some day, Pastor: Uncle William used to drink before breakfast. Come: it will give your sermons unction. [*He smells the wine and makes a wry face.*] But do not begin on my mother's company sherry. I stole some when I was six years old; and I have been a temperate man ever since. [*He puts the decanter down and changes the subject.*] So I hear you are married, Pastor, and that your wife has a most ungodly allowance of good looks.

ANDERSON. [*quietly indicating JUDITH*]. Sir: you are in the presence of my wife. [*JUDITH rises and stands with stony propriety.*]

RICHARD. [*quickly slipping down from the table with instinctive good manners*]. Your servant, madam: no offence. [*He looks at her earnestly.*] You deserve your reputation; but I'm sorry to see by your expression that you're a good woman. [*She looks shocked, and sits down amid a murmur of indignant sympathy from his relatives. ANDERSON, sensible enough to know that these demonstrations can only gratify and encourage a man who is deliberately trying to provoke them, remains perfectly goodhumored.*] All the same, Pastor, I respect you more than I did before. By the way, did I hear, or did I not, that our late lamented Uncle Peter, though unmarried, was a father?

UNCLE TITUS. He had only one irregular child, sir.

RICHARD. Only one! He thinks one a mere trifle! I blush for you, Uncle Titus.

ANDERSON. Mr. Dudgeon you are in the presence of your mother and her grief.

RICHARD. It touches me profoundly, Pastor. By the way, what has become of the irregular child?

ANDERSON. [*pointing to ESSIE*]. There, sir, listening to you.

RICHARD. [*shocked into sincerity*]. What! Why the devil didn't you tell me that before? Children suffer enough in this house without—[*He hurries remorsefully to ESSIE.*] Come, little cousin! never mind me: it was not meant to hurt you. [*She looks up gratefully at him. Her tearstained face affects him violently, and he bursts out, in a transport of wrath*] Who has been making her cry? Who has been ill-treating her? By God—

MRS. DUDGEON. [*rising and confronting him*]. Silence your blasphemous tongue. I will hear no more of this. Leave my house.

RICHARD. How do you know it's your house until the will is read? [*They look at one another for a moment with intense hatred; and then she sinks, checkmated, into her chair. RICHARD goes boldly up past ANDERSON to the window, where he takes the railed chair in his hand.*] Ladies and gentlemen: as the eldest son of my late father, and the unworthy head of this household, I bid you welcome. By your leave, Minister Anderson: by your leave, Lawyer Hawkins. The head of the table for the head of the family. [*He places the chair at the table between the minister and the attorney; sits down between them; and addresses the assembly with a presidential air.*] We meet on a melancholy occasion: a father dead! an uncle actually hanged, and probably damned. [*He shakes his head deploringly. The relatives freeze with horror.*] That's right: pull your longest faces [*his voice suddenly sweetens gravely as his glance lights on ESSIE*] provided only there is hope in the eyes of the child. [*Briskly.*] Now then, Lawyer Hawkins: business, business. Get on with the will, man.

TITUS. Do not let yourself be ordered or hurried, Mr. Hawkins.

HAWKINS. [*very politely and willingly*]. Mr. Dudgeon means no offence, I feel sure. I will not keep you one second, Mr. Dudgeon. Just while I get my glasses—[*he fumbles for them. The DUDGEONS look at one another with misgiving*].

RICHARD. Aha! They notice your civility, Mr. Hawkins. They are prepared for the worst. A glass of wine to clear your voice before you begin. [*He pours out one for him and hands it; then pours one for himself.*]

HAWKINS. Thank you, Mr. Dudgeon. Your good health, sir.

RICHARD. Yours, sir. [*With the glass half way to his lips, he checks himself, giving a dubious glance at the wine, and adds, with quaint intensity.*] Will anyone oblige me with a glass of water?

ESSIE, who has been hanging on his every word and movement, rises stealthily and slips out behind MRS. DUDGEON through the bedroom door, returning presently with a jug and going out of the house as quietly as possible.

HAWKINS. The will is not exactly in proper legal phraseology.

RICHARD. No: my father died without the consolations of the law.

HAWKINS. Good again, Mr. Dudgeon, good again. [*Preparing to read*] Are you ready, sir?

RICHARD. Ready, aye ready. For what we are about to receive, may the Lord make us truly thankful. Go ahead.

HAWKINS. [*reading*]. "This is the last will and testament of me Timothy Dudgeon on my deathbed at Nevinstown on the road from Springtown to Websterbridge on this twenty-fourth day of September, one thousand seven hundred and seventy seven. I hereby revoke all former wills made by me and declare that I am of sound mind and know well what I am doing and that this is my real will according to my own wish and affections."

RICHARD. [*glancing at his mother*]. Aha!

HAWKINS. [*shaking his head*]. Bad phraseology, sir, wrong phraseology. "I give and bequeath a hundred pounds to my younger son Christopher Dudgeon, fifty pounds to be paid to him on the day of his marriage to Sarah Wilkins if she will have him, and ten pounds on the birth of each of his children up to the number of five."

RICHARD. How if she won't have him?

CHRISTY. She will if I have fifty pounds.

RICHARD. Good, my brother. Proceed.

HAWKINS. "I give and bequeath to my wife Annie Dudgeon, born Annie Primrose"—you see he did not know the law, Mr. Dudgeon: your mother was not born Annie: she was christened so—"an annuity of fifty-two pounds a year for life [*MRS. DUDGEON, with all eyes on her, holds herself convulsively rigid*] to be paid out of the interest on her own money"—there's a way to put it, Mr. Dudgeon! Her own money!

MRS. DUDGEON. A very good way to put God's truth. It was every penny my own. Fifty-two pounds a year!

HAWKINS. "And I recommend her for her goodness and piety to the forgiving care of her children, having stood between them and her as far as I could to the best of my ability."

MRS. DUDGEON. And this is my reward! [*raging inwardly*] You know what I think, Mr. Anderson you know the word I gave to it.

ANDERSON. It cannot be helped, Mrs. Dudgeon. We must take what comes to us. [*To HAWKINS.*] Go on, sir.

HAWKINS. "I give and bequeath my house at Websterbridge with the land belonging to it and all the rest of my property soever to my eldest son and heir, Richard Dudgeon."

RICHARD. Oho! The fatted calf, Minister, the fatted calf.

HAWKINS. "On these conditions—"

RICHARD. The devil! Are there conditions?

HAWKINS. "To wit: first, that he shall not let my brother Peter's natural child starve or be driven by want to an evil life."

RICHARD. [*emphatically, striking his fist on the table*]. Agreed. *MRS. DUDGEON, turning to look malignantly at ESSIE, misses her and looks quickly round to see where she has moved to; then, seeing that she has left the room without leave, closes her lips vengefully.*

HAWKINS. "Second, that he shall be a good friend to my old horse Jim"—[*again slacking his head*] he should have written James, sir.

RICHARD. James shall live in clover. Go on.

HAWKINS. "—and keep my deaf farm laborer Prodger Feston in his service."

RICHARD. Prodger Feston shall get drunk every Saturday.

HAWKINS. "Third, that he make Christy a present on his marriage out of the ornaments in the best room."

RICHARD. [*holding up the stuffed birds*]. Here you are, Christy.

CHRISTY. [*disappointed*]. I'd rather have the China peacocks.

RICHARD. You shall have both. [*CHRISTY is greatly pleased.*] Go on.

HAWKINS. "Fourthly and lastly, that he try to live at peace with his mother as far as she will consent to it."

RICHARD. [*dubiously*]. Hm! Anything more, Mr. Hawkins?

HAWKINS. [*solemnly*]. "Finally I gave and bequeath my soul into my Maker's hands, humbly asking forgiveness for all my sins and mistakes, and hoping that he will so guide my son that it may not be said that I have done wrong in trusting to him rather than to others in the perplexity of my last hour in this strange place."

ANDERSON. Amen.

THE UNCLES AND AUNTS. Amen.

RICHARD. My mother does not say Amen.

MRS. DUDGEON. [*rising, unable to give up her property without a struggle*]. Mr. Hawkins: is that a proper will? Remember, I have his rightful, legal will, drawn up by yourself, leaving all to me.

HAWKINS. This is a very wrongly and irregularly worded will, Mrs. Dudgeon; though [*turning politely to RICHARD*] it contains in my judgment an excellent disposal of his property.

ANDERSON. [*interposing before MRS. DUDGEON can retort*]. That is not what you are asked, Mr. Hawkins. Is it a legal will?

HAWKINS. The courts will sustain it against the other.

ANDERSON. But why, if the other is more lawfully worded?

HAWKING. Because, sir, the courts will sustain the claim of a man—and that man the eldest son—against any woman, if they can. I warned you, Mrs. Dudgeon, when you got me to draw that other will, that it was not a wise will, and that though you might make him sign it, he would never be easy until he revoked it. But you wouldn't take advice; and now Mr. Richard is cock of the walk. [*He takes his hat from the floor; rises; and begins pocketing his papers and spectacles.*]

This is the signal for the breaking-up of the party. ANDERSON takes his hat from the rack and joins UNCLE WILLIAM at the fire. UNCLE TITUS fetches JUDITH her things from the rack. The three on the sofa rise and chat with HAWKINS. MRS. DUDGEON, now an intruder in her own house, stands erect, crushed by the weight of the law on women, accepting it, as she has been trained to accept all monstrous calamities, as proofs of the greatness of the power that inflicts them, and of her own wormlike insignificance. For at this time, remember, Mary Wollstonecraft is as yet only a girl of eighteen, and her Vindication of the Rights of Women is still fourteen years off. MRS. DUDGEON is rescued from her apathy by ESSIE, who comes back with the jug full of water. She is taking it to RICHARD when MRS. DUDGEON stops her.

MRS. DUDGEON. [*threatening her*]. Where have you been? [*ESSIE, appalled, tries to answer, but cannot.*] How dare you go out by yourself after the orders I gave you?

ESSIE. He asked for a drink—[*she stops, her tongue cleaving to her palate with terror*].

JUDITH. [with gentler severity]. Who asked for a drink? [*ESSIE, speechless, points to RICHARD.*]

RICHARD. What! I!

JUDITH. [*shocked*]. Oh Essie, Essie!

RICHARD. I believe I did. [*He takes a glass and holds it to ESSIE to be filled. Her hand shakes.*] What! afraid of me?

ESSIE. [quickly]. No. I—[*She pours out the water.*]

RICHARD. [tasting it]. Ah, you've been up the street to the market gate spring to get that. [*He takes a draught.*] Delicious! Thank you. [*Unfortunately, at this moment he chances to catch sight of JUDITH's face, which expresses the most prudish disapproval of his evident attraction for ESSIE, who is devouring him with her grateful eyes. His mocking expression returns instantly. He puts down the glass; deliberately winds his arm round ESSIE's shoulders; and brings her into the middle of the company. MRS. DUDGEON being in ESSIE's way as they come past the table, he says*] By your leave, mother [*and compels her to make way for them*]. What do they call you? Bessie?

ESSIE. Essie.

RICHARD. Essie, to be sure. Are you a good girl, Essie?

ESSIE. [*greatly disappointed that he, of all people should begin at her in this way*] Yes. [*She looks doubtfully at JUDITH.*] I think so. I mean I—I hope so.

RICHARD. Essie: did you ever hear of a person called the devil?

ANDERSON. [*revolted*]. Shame on you, sir, with a mere child—

RICHARD. By your leave, Minister: I do not interfere with your sermons: do not you interrupt mine. [*To ESSIE.*] Do you know what they call me, Essie?

ESSIE. Dick.

RICHARD. [*amused: patting her on the shoulder*]. Yes, Dick; but something else too. They call me the Devil's Disciple.

ESSIE. Why do you let them?

RICHARD. [*seriously*]. Because it's true. I was brought up in the other service; but I knew from the first that the Devil was my natural master and captain and friend. I saw that he was in the right, and that the world cringed to his conqueror only through fear. I prayed secretly to him; and he comforted me, and saved me from having my spirit broken in this house of children's tears. I promised him my soul, and swore an oath that I would stand up for him in this world and stand by him in the next. [*Solemnly*] That promise and that oath made a man of me. From this day this house is his home; and no child shall cry in it: this hearth is his altar; and no soul shall ever cower over it in the dark evenings and be afraid. Now [*turning forcibly on the rest*] which of you good men will take this child and rescue her from the house of the devil?

JUDITH. [*coming to ESSIE and throwing a protecting arm about her*]. I will. You should be burnt alive.

ESSIE. But I don't want to. [*She shrinks back, leaving RICHARD and JUDITH face to face.*]

RICHARD. [*to JUDITH*]. Actually doesn't want to, most virtuous lady!

UNCLE TITUS. Have a care, Richard Dudgeon. The law—

RICHARD. [*turning threateningly on him*]. Have a care, you. In an hour from this there will be no law here but martial law. I passed the soldiers within six miles on my way here: before noon Major Swindon's gallows for rebels will be up in the market place.

ANDERSON. [*calmly*]. What have we to fear from that, sir?

RICHARD. More than you think. He hanged the wrong man at Springtown: he thought Uncle Peter was respectable, because the Dudgeons had a good name. But his next example will be the best man in the town to whom he can bring home a rebellious word. Well, we're all rebels; and you know it.

ALL. THE MEN [*except ANDERSON*]. No, no, no!

RICHARD. Yes, you are. You haven't damned King George up hill and down dale as I have; but you've prayed for his defeat; and you, Anthony Anderson, have conducted the service, and sold your family bible to buy a pair of pistols. They mayn't hang me, perhaps; because the moral effect of the Devil's Disciple dancing on nothing wouldn't help them. But a Minister! [*JUDITH, dismayed, clings to ANDERSON*] or a lawyer! [*HAWKINS smiles like a man able to take care of himself*] or an upright horsedealer! [*UNCLE TITUS snarls at him in rags and terror*] or a reformed drunkard [*UNCLE*

WILLIAM, utterly unnerved, moans and wobbles with fear]
eh? Would that show that King George meant business—ha?

ANDERSON. [*perfectly self-possessed*]. Come, my dear: he is
only trying to frighten you. There is no danger. [*He takes her
out of the house. The rest crowd to the door to follow him,
except ESSIE, who remains near RICHARD.*]

RICHARD. [*boisterously derisive*]. Now then: how many of you
will stay with me; run up the American flag on the devil's
house; and make a fight for freedom? [*They scramble out,
CHRISTY among them, hustling one another in their haste.*]
Ha ha! Long live the devil! [*To MRS. DUDGEON, who is
following them*] What mother! are you off too?

MRS. DUDGEON. [*deadly pale, with her hand on her heart as
if she had received a deathblow*]. My curse on you! My
dying curse! [*She goes out.*]

RICHARD. [*calling after her*]. It will bring me luck. Ha ha ha!

ESSIE. [*anxiously*]. Mayn't I stay?

RICHARD. [*turning to her*]. What! Have they forgotten to save
your soul in their anxiety about their own bodies? Oh yes:
you may stay. [*He turns excitedly away again and shakes his
fist after them. His left fist, also clenched, hangs down.
ESSIE seizes it and kisses it, her tears falling on it. He starts
and looks at it.*] Tears! The devil's baptism! [*She falls on her
knees, sobbing. He stoops goodnaturedly to raise her,
saying*] Oh yes, you may cry that way, Essie, if you like.

ACT II

Minister Anderson's house is in the main street of Websterbridge, not far from the town hall. To the eye of the eighteenth century New Englander, it is much grander than the plain farmhouse of the Dudgeons; but it is so plain itself that a modern house agent would let both at about the same rent. The chief dwelling room has the same sort of kitchen fireplace, with boiler, toaster hanging on the bars, movable iron griddle socketed to the hob, hook above for roasting, and broad fender, on which stand a kettle and a plate of buttered toast. The door, between the fireplace and the corner, has neither panels, fingerplates nor handles: it is made of plain boards, and fastens with a latch. The table is a kitchen table, with a treacle colored cover of American cloth, chapped at the corners by draping. The tea service on it consists of two thick cups and saucers of the plainest ware, with milk jug and bowl to match, each large enough to contain nearly a quart, on a black japanned tray, and, in the middle of the table, a wooden trencher with a big loaf upon it, and a square half pound block of butter in a crock. The big oak press facing the fire from the opposite side of the room, is for use and storage, not for ornament; and the minister's house coat hangs on a peg from its door, showing that he is out; for when he is in it is his best coat that hangs there. His big riding boots stand beside the press, evidently in their usual place, and rather proud of themselves. In fact, the evolution of the minister's kitchen, dining room and drawing room into three separate apartments has not yet taken place; and so, from the point of view of our pampered period, he is no better off than the Dudgeons.

But there is a difference, for all that. To begin with, Mrs. Anderson is a pleasanter person to live with than Mrs. Dudgeon. To which Mrs. Dudgeon would at once reply, with reason, that Mrs. Anderson has no children to look after; no poultry, pigs nor cattle; a steady and sufficient income not directly dependent on harvests and prices at fairs; an affectionate husband who is a tower of strength to her: in short, that life is as easy at the minister's house as it is hard at the farm. This is true; but to explain a fact is not to alter it; and however little credit Mrs. Anderson may deserve for making her home happier, she has certainly succeeded in doing it. The outward and visible signs of her superior social pretensions are a drugget on the floor, a plaster ceiling between the timbers and chairs which, though not upholstered, are stained and polished. The fine arts are represented by a mezzotint portrait of some Presbyterian divine, a copperplate of Raphael's St. Paul preaching at Athens, a rococo presentation clock on the mantelshelf, flanked by a couple of miniatures, a pair of crockery dogs with baskets in their mouths, and, at the corners, two large cowrie shells. A pretty feature of the room is the low wide latticed window, nearly its whole width, with little red curtains running on a rod half way up it to serve as a blind. There is no sofa; but one of the seats, standing near the press, has a railed back and is long enough to accommodate two people easily. On the whole, it is rather the sort of room that the nineteenth century has ended in struggling to get back to under the leadership of Mr. Philip Webb and his disciples in domestic architecture, though no genteel clergyman would have tolerated it fifty years ago.

The evening has closed in; and the room is dark except for the cosy firelight and the dim oil lamps seen through the window in the wet street, where there is a quiet, steady, warm, windless downpour of rain. As the town clock strikes the quarter, Judith comes in with a couple of candles in earthenware candlesticks, and sets them on the table. Her self-conscious airs of the morning are gone: she is anxious and frightened. She goes to the window and peers into the street. The first thing she sees there is her husband, hurrying here through the rain.

She gives a little gasp of relief, not very far removed from a sob, and turns to the door. Anderson comes in, wrapped in a very wet cloak.

JUDITH. [*running to him*]. Oh, here you are at last, at last! [*She attempts to embrace him.*]

ANDERSON. [*keeping her off*]. Take care, my love: I'm wet. Wait till I get my cloak off. [*He places a chair with its back to the fire; hangs his cloak on it to dry; shakes the rain from his hat and puts it on the fender; and at last turns with his hands outstretched to JUDITH.*] Now! [*She flies into his arms.*] I am not late, am I? The town clock struck the quarter as I came in at the front door. And the town clock is always fast.

JUDITH. I'm sure it's slow this evening. I'm so glad you're back.

ANDERSON. [*taking her more closely in his arms*]. Anxious, my dear?

JUDITH. A little.

ANDERSON. Why, you've been crying.

JUDITH. Only a little. Never mind: it's all over now. [*A bugle call is heard in the distance. She starts in terror and retreats to the long seat, listening.*] What's that?

ANDERSON. [*following her tenderly to the seat and making her sit down with him*]. Only King George, my dear. He's returning to barracks, or having his roll called, or getting ready for tea, or booting or saddling or something. Soldiers don't ring the bell or call over the banisters when they want anything: they send a boy out with a bugle to disturb the whole town.

JUDITH. Do you think there is really any danger?

ANDERSON. Not the least in the world.

JUDITH. You say that to comfort me, not because you believe it.

ANDERSON. My dear: in this world there is always danger for those who are afraid of it. There's a danger that the house will catch fire in the night; but we shan't sleep any the less soundly for that.

JUDITH. Yes, I know what you always say; and you're quite right. Oh, quite right: I know it. But—I suppose I'm not brave: that's all. My heart shrinks every time I think of the soldiers.

ANDERSON. Never mind that, dear: bravery is none the worse for costing a little pain.

JUDITH. Yes, I suppose so. [*Embracing him again.*] Oh how brave you are, my dear! [*With tears in her eyes.*] Well, I'll be brave too: you shan't be ashamed of your wife.

ANDERSON. That's right. Now you make me happy. Well, well! [*He rises and goes cheerily to the fire to dry his shoes.*] I called on Richard Dudgeon on my way back; but he wasn't in.

JUDITH. [*rising in consternation*]. You called on that man!

ANDERSON. [*reassuring her*]. Oh, nothing happened, dearie. He was out.

JUDITH. [*almost in tears, as if the visit were a personal humiliation to her*]. But why did you go there?

ANDERSON. [*gravely*]. Well, it is all the talk that Major Swindon is going to do what he did in Springtown—make an example of some notorious rebel, as he calls us. He pounced on Peter Dudgeon as the worst character there; and it is the general belief that he will pounce on Richard as the worst here.

JUDITH. But Richard said—

ANDERSON. [*goodhumoredly cutting her short*]. Pooh! Richard said! He said what he thought would frighten you and frighten me, my dear. He said what perhaps [*God forgive him!*] he would like to believe. It's a terrible thing to think of what death must mean for a man like that. I felt that I must warn him. I left a message for him.

JUDITH. [*querulously*]. What message?

ANDERSON. Only that I should be glad to see him for a moment on a matter of importance to himself; and that if he would look in here when he was passing he would be welcome.

JUDITH. [*aghast*]. You asked that man to come here!

ANDERSON. I did.

JUDITH. [*sinking on the seat and clasping her hands*]. I hope he won't come! Oh, I pray that he may not come!

ANDERSON. Why? Don't you want him to be warned?

JUDITH. He must know his danger. Oh, Tony, is it wrong to hate a blasphemer and a villain? I do hate him! I can't get him out of my mind: I know he will bring harm with him. He insulted you: he insulted me: he insulted his mother.

ANDERSON. [*quaintly*]. Well, dear, let's forgive him; and then it won't matter.

JUDITH. Oh, I know it's wrong to hate anybody; but—

ANDERSON. [*going over to her with humorous tenderness*]. Come, dear, you're not so wicked as you think. The worst sin towards our fellow creatures is not to hate them, but to be indifferent to them: that's the essence of inhumanity. After all, my dear, if you watch people carefully, you'll be surprised to find how like hate is to love. [She starts, strangely touched—even appalled. He is amused at her.] Yes: I'm quite in earnest. Think of how some of our married friends worry one another, tax one another, are jealous of one another, can't bear to let one another out of sight for a day, are more like jailers and slave-owners than lovers. Think of those very same people with their enemies, scrupulous, lofty, self-respecting, determined to be independent of one another, careful of how they speak of one another—pooh! haven't you often thought that if they only knew it, they were better friends to their enemies than to their own husbands and wives? Come: depend on it, my dear, you are really fonder of Richard than you are of me, if you only knew it. Eh?

JUDITH. Oh, don't say that: don't say that, Tony, even in jest. You don't know what a horrible feeling it gives me.

ANDERSON. [*Laughing*]. Well, well: never mind, pet. He's a bad man; and you hate him as he deserves. And you're going to make the tea, aren't you?

JUDITH. [*remorsefully*]. Oh yes, I forgot. I've been keeping you waiting all this time. [She goes to the fire and puts on the kettle.]

ANDERSON. [*going to the press and taking his coat off*]. Have you stitched up the shoulder of my old coat?

JUDITH. Yes, dear. [*She goes to the table, and sets about putting the tea into the teapot from the caddy.*]

ANDERSON. [*as he changes his coat for the older one hanging on the press, and replaces it by the one he has just taken off*]. Did anyone call when I was out?

JUDITH. No, only—[*someone knocks at the door. With a start which betrays her intense nervousness, she retreats to the further end of the table with the tea caddy and spoon, in her hands, exclaiming*] Who's that?

ANDERSON. [*going to her and patting her encouragingly on the shoulder*]. All right, pet, all right. He won't eat you, whoever he is. [*She tries to smile, and nearly makes herself cry. He goes to the door and opens it. RICHARD is there, without overcoat or cloak.*] You might have raised the latch and come in, Mr. Dudgeon. Nobody stands on much ceremony with us. [*Hospitably.*] Come in. [*RICHARD comes in carelessly and stands at the table, looking round the room with a slight pucker of his nose at the mezzotinted divine on the wall. JUDITH keeps her eyes on the tea caddy.*] Is it still raining? [*He shuts the door.*]

RICHARD. Raining like the very [*his eye catches JUDITH's as she looks quickly and haughtily up*]—I beg your pardon; but [showing that his coat is wet] you see—!

ANDERSON. Take it off, sir; and let it hang before the fire a while: my wife will excuse your shirtsleeves. Judith: put in another spoonful of tea for Mr. Dudgeon.

RICHARD. [*eyeing him cynically*]. The magic of property, Pastor! Are even *you* civil to me now that I have succeeded to my father's estate?

[*JUDITH throws down the spoon indignantly.*]

ANDERSON. [*quite unruffled, and helping RICHARD off with his coat*]. I think, sir, that since you accept my hospitality, you cannot have so bad an opinion of it. Sit down. [*With the coat in his hand, he points to the railed seat. RICHARD, in his shirtsleeves, looks at him half quarrelsomely for a moment; then, with a nod, acknowledges that the minister has got the better of him, and sits down on the seat. ANDERSON pushes his cloak into a heap on the seat of the chair at the fire, and hangs RICHARD's coat on the back in its place.*]

RICHARD. I come, sir, on your own invitation. You left word you had something important to tell me.

ANDERSON. I have a warning which it is my duty to give you.

RICHARD. [*quickly rising*]. You want to preach to me. Excuse me: I prefer a walk in the rain. [*He makes for his coat.*]

ANDERSON. [*stopping him*]. Don't be alarmed, sir; I am no great preacher. You are quite safe. [*RICHARD smiles in spite of himself. His glance softens: he even makes a gesture of excuse. ANDERSON, seeing that he has tamed him, now addresses him earnestly.*] Mr. Dudgeon: you are in danger in this town.

RICHARD. What danger?

ANDERSON. Your uncle's danger. Major Swindon's gallows.

RICHARD. It is you who are in danger. I warned you—

ANDERSON. [*interrupting him goodhumoredly but authoritatively*]. Yes, yes, Mr. Dudgeon; but they do not think so in the town. And even if I were in danger, I have duties here I must not forsake. But you are a free man. Why should you run any risk?

RICHARD. Do you think I should be any great loss, Minister?

ANDERSON. I think that a man's life is worth saving, whoever it belongs to. [*RICHARD makes him an ironical bow. ANDERSON returns the bow humorously.*] Come: you'll have a cup of tea, to prevent you catching cold?

RICHARD. I observe that Mrs. Anderson is not quite so pressing as you are, Pastor.

JUDITH. [*almost stifled with resentment, which she has been expecting her husband to share and express for her at every insult of RICHARD's*]. You are welcome for my husband's sake. [*She brings the teapot to the fireplace and sets it on the hob.*]

RICHARD. I know I am not welcome for my own, madam. [*He rises.*] But I think I will not break bread here, Minister.

ANDERSON. [*cheerily*]. Give me a good reason for that.

RICHARD. Because there is something in you that I respect, and that makes me desire to have you for my enemy.

ANDERSON. That's well said. On those terms, sir, I will accept your enmity or any man's. Judith: Mr. Dudgeon will stay to tea. Sit down: it will take a few minutes to draw by the fire. [*RICHARD glances at him with a troubled face; then sits down with his head bent, to hide a convulsive swelling of his throat.*] I was just saying to my wife, Mr. Dudgeon, that enmity—[*she grasps his hand and looks imploringly at him, doing both with an intensity that checks him at once*] Well, well, I mustn't tell you, I see; but it was nothing that need leave us worse friend—enemies, I mean. Judith is a great enemy of yours.

RICHARD. If all my enemies were like Mrs. Anderson I should be the best Christian in America.

ANDERSON. [*gratified, patting her hand*]. You hear that, Judith? Mr. Dudgeon knows how to turn a compliment.

[*The latch is lifted from without.*]

JUDITH. [*starting*]. Who is that?

Christy comes in.

CHRISTY. [*stopping and staring at RICHARD*]. Oh, are *you* here?

RICHARD. Yes. Begone, you fool: Mrs. Anderson doesn't want the whole family to tea at once.

CHRISTY. [*coming further in*]. Mother's very ill.

RICHARD. Well, does she want to see *me*?

CHRISTY. No.

RICHARD. I thought not.

CHRISTY. She wants to see the minister—at once.

JUDITH. [*to ANDERSON*]. Oh, not before you've had some tea.

ANDERSON. I shall enjoy it more when I come back, dear. [He is about to take up his cloak.]

CHRISTY. The rain's over.

ANDERSON. [*dropping the cloak and picking up his hat from the fender*]. Where is your mother, Christy?

CHRISTY. At Uncle Titus's.

ANDERSON. Have you fetched the doctor?

CHRISTY. No: she didn't tell me to.

ANDERSON. Go on there at once: I'll overtake you on his doorstep. [*CHRISTY turns to go.*] Wait a moment. Your brother must be anxious to know the particulars.

RICHARD. Psha! not I: he doesn't know; and I don't care. [*Violently.*] Be off, you oaf. [*CHRISTY runs out. RICHARD adds, a little shamefacedly*] We shall know soon enough.

ANDERSON. Well, perhaps you will let me bring you the news myself. Judith: will you give Mr. Dudgeon his tea, and keep him here until I return?

JUDITH. [*white and trembling*]. Must I—

ANDERSON. [*taking her hands and interrupting her to cover her agitation*]. My dear: I can depend on you?

JUDITH. [*with a piteous effort to be worthy of his trust*]. Yes.

ANDERSON. [*pressing her hand against his cheek*]. You will not mind two old people like us, Mr. Dudgeon. [*Going.*] I shall not say good evening: you will be here when I come back. [*He goes out.*]

They watch him pass the window, and then look at each other dumbly, quite disconcerted. RICHARD, noting the quiver of her lips, is the first to pull himself together.

RICHARD. Mrs. Anderson: I am perfectly aware of the nature of your sentiments towards me. I shall not intrude on you. Good evening. [*Again he starts for the fireplace to get his coat.*]

JUDITH. [*getting between him and the coat*]. No, no. Don't go: please don't go.

RICHARD. [*roughly*]. Why? You don't want me here.

JUDITH. Yes, I—[*wringing her hands in despair*] Oh, if I tell you the truth, you will use it to torment me.

RICHARD. [*indignantly*]. Torment! What right have you to say that? Do you expect me to stay after that?

JUDITH. I want you to stay; but [*suddenly raging at him like an angry child*] it is not because I like you.

RICHARD. Indeed!

JUDITH. Yes: I had rather you did go than mistake me about that. I hate and dread you; and my husband knows it. If you are not here when he comes back, he will believe that I disobeyed him and drove you away.

RICHARD. [*ironically*]. Whereas, of course, you have really been so kind and hospitable and charming to me that I only want to go away out of mere contrariness, eh?

[*JUDITH, unable to bear it, sinks on the chair and bursts into tears.*]

RICHARD. Stop, stop, stop, I tell you. Don't do that. [*Putting his hand to his breast as if to a wound.*] He wrung my heart by being a man. Need you tear it by being a woman? Has he not raised you above my insults, like himself? [*She stops crying, and recovers herself somewhat, looking at him with a scared curiosity.*] There: that's right. [*Sympathetically.*] You're better now, aren't you? [*He puts his hand encouragingly on her shoulder. She instantly rises haughtily, and stares at him defiantly. He at once drops into his usual sardonic tone.*] Ah, that's better. You are yourself again: so is Richard. Well, shall we go to tea like a quiet respectable couple, and wait for your husband's return?

JUDITH. [*rather ashamed of herself*]. If you please. I—I am sorry to have been so foolish. [*She stoops to take up the plate of toast from the fender.*]

RICHARD. I am sorry, for your sake, that I am—what I am. Allow me. [*He takes the plate from her and goes with it to the table.*]

JUDITH. [*following with the teapot*]. Will you sit down? [*He sits down at the end of the table nearest the press. There is a plate and knife laid there. The other plate is laid near it; but JUDITH stays at the opposite end of the table, next the fire, and takes her place there, drawing the tray towards her.*] Do you take sugar?

RICHARD. No; but plenty of milk. Let me give you some toast. [*He puts some on the second plate, and hands it to her, with the knife. The action shows quietly how well he knows that she has avoided her usual place so as to be as far from him as possible.*]

JUDITH. [*consciously*]. Thanks. [*She gives him his tea.*] Won't you help yourself?

RICHARD. Thanks. [*He puts a piece of toast on his own plate; and she pours out tea for herself.*]

JUDITH. [*observing that he tastes nothing*]. Don't you like it? You are not eating anything.

RICHARD. Neither are you.

JUDITH. [*nervously*]. I never care much for my tea. Please don't mind me.

RICHARD. [*Looking dreamily round*]. I am thinking. It is all so strange to me. I can see the beauty and peace of this home: I think I have never been more at rest in my life than at this moment; and yet I know quite well I could never live here. It's not in my nature, I suppose, to be domesticated. But it's very beautiful: it's almost holy. [*He muses a moment, and then laughs softly.*]

JUDITH. [*quickly*]. Why do you laugh?

RICHARD. I was thinking that if any stranger came in here now, he would take us for man and wife.

JUDITH. [*taking offence*]. You mean, I suppose, that you are more my age than he is.

RICHARD. [*staring at this unexpected turn*]. I never thought of such a thing. [*Sardonic again.*] I see there is another side to domestic joy.

JUDITH. [*angrily*]. I would rather have a husband whom everybody respects than—than—

RICHARD. Than the devil's disciple. You are right; but I daresay your love helps him to be a good man, just as your hate helps me to be a bad one.

JUDITH. My husband has been very good to you. He has forgiven you for insulting him, and is trying to save you. Can you not forgive him for being so much better than you are? How dare you belittle him by putting yourself in his place?

RICHARD. Did I?

JUDITH. Yes, you did. You said that if anybody came in they would take us for man and—[*she stops, terror-stricken, as a squad of soldiers tramps past the window*] The English soldiers! Oh, what do they—

RICHARD. [*listening*]. Sh!

A VOICE. [*outside*]. Halt! Four outside: two in with me.

JUDITH half rises, listening and looking with dilated eyes at RICHARD, who takes up his cup prosaically, and is drinking his tea when the latch goes up with a sharp click, and an English sergeant walks into the room with two privates, who post themselves at the door. He comes promptly to the table between them.

THE SERGEANT. Sorry to disturb you, mum! duty! Anthony Anderson: I arrest you in King George's name as a rebel.

JUDITH. [*pointing at RICHARD*]. But that is not—[*He looks up quickly at her, with a face of iron. She stops her mouth hastily with the hand she has raised to indicate him, and stands staring affrightedly.*]

THE SERGEANT. Come, Parson; put your coat on and come along.

RICHARD. Yes: I'll come. [*He rises and takes a step towards his own coat; then recollects himself, and, with his back to the sergeant, moves his gaze slowly round the room without turning his head until he sees ANDERSON's black coat hanging up on the press. He goes composedly to it; takes it down; and puts it on. The idea of himself as a parson tickles him: he looks down at the black sleeve on his arm, and then smiles slyly at JUDITH, whose white face shows him that what she is painfully struggling to grasp is not the humor of the situation but its horror. He turns to the sergeant, who is approaching him with a pair of handcuffs hidden behind him, and says lightly*] Did you ever arrest a man of my cloth before, Sergeant?

THE SERGEANT. [*instinctively respectful, half to the black coat, half to RICHARD's good breeding*]. Well, no sir. At least, only an army chaplain. [*Showing the handcuffs.*] I'm sorry, air; but duty—

RICHARD. Just so, Sergeant. Well, I'm not ashamed of them: thank you kindly for the apology. [*He holds out his hands.*]

SERGEANT. [*not availing himself of the offer*]. One gentleman to another, sir. Wouldn't you like to say a word to your missis, sir, before you go?

RICHARD. [*smiling*]. Oh, we shall meet again before—eh? [*Meaning "before you hang me."*]

SERGEANT. [loudly, with ostentatious cheerfulness]. Oh, of course, of course. No call for the lady to distress herself.

Still—[in a lower voice, intended for Richard alone] your last chance, sir.

They look at one another significantly for a moment. Than RICHARD exhales a deep breath and turns towards JUDITH.

RICHARD. [*very distinctly*]. My love. [*She looks at him, pitiably pale, and tries to answer, but cannot—tries also to come to him, but cannot trust herself to stand without the support of the table.*] This gallant gentleman is good enough to allow us a moment of leavetaking. [*The SERGEANT retires delicately and joins his men near the door.*] He is trying to spare you the truth; but you had better know it. Are you listening to me? [*She signifies assent.*] Do you understand that I am going to my death? [*She signifies that she understands.*] Remember, you must find our friend who was with us just now. Do you understand? [*She signifies yes.*] See that you get him safely out of harm's way. Don't for your life let him know of my danger; but if he finds it out, tell him that he cannot save me: they would hang him; and they would not spare me. And tell him that I am steadfast in my religion as he is in his, and that he may depend on me to the death. [*He turns to go, and meets the eye of the SERGEANT, who looks a little suspicious. He considers a moment, and then, turning roguishly to JUDITH with something of a smile breaking through his earnestness, says*] And now, my dear, I am afraid the sergeant will not believe that you love me like a wife unless you give one kiss before I go.

He approaches her and holds out his arms. She quits the table and almost falls into them.

JUDITH. [*the words choking her*]. I ought to—it's murder—

RICHARD. No: only a kiss [*softly to her*] for his sake.

JUDITH. I can't. You must—

RICHARD. [*folding her in his arms with an impulse of compassion for her distress*]. My poor girl!

JUDITH, with a sudden effort, throws her arms round him; kisses him; and swoons away, dropping from his arms to the ground as if the kiss had killed her.

RICHARD. [*going quickly to the SERGEANT*]. Now, Sergeant: quick, before she comes to. The handcuffs. [*He puts out his hands.*]

SERGEANT. [*pocketing them*]. Never mind, sir: I'll trust you. You're a game one. You ought to a bin a soldier, sir. Between them two, please. [*The soldiers place themselves one before RICHARD and one behind him. The sergeant opens the door.*]

RICHARD. [*taking a last look round him*]. Goodbye, wife: goodbye, home. Muffle the drums, and quick march!

The sergeant signs to the leading soldier to march. They file out quickly.

***********************When ANDERSON returns from MRS. DUDGEON's he is astonished to find the room apparently empty and almost in darkness except for the glow from the fire; for one of the candles has burnt out, and the other is at its last flicker.*

ANDERSON. Why, what on earth—? [*Calling*] Judith, Judith! [*He listens: there is no answer.*] Hm! [*He goes to the cupboard; takes a candle from the drawer; lights it at the flicker of the expiring one on the table; and looks wonderingly at the untasted meal by its light. Then he sticks it in the candlestick; takes off his hat; and scratches his head, much puzzled. This action causes him to look at the floor for the first time; and there he sees JUDITH lying motionless with her eyes closed. He runs to her and stoops beside her, lifting her head.*] Judith.

JUDITH. [*waking; for her swoon has passed into the sleep of exhaustion after suffering*]. Yes. Did you call? What's the matter?

ANDERSON. I've just come in and found you lying here with the candles burnt out and the tea poured out and cold. What has happened?

JUDITH. [still astray]. I don't know. Have I been asleep? I suppose—[*she stops blankly*] I don't know.

ANDERSON. [*groaning*]. Heaven forgive me, I left you alone with that scoundrel. [*JUDITH remembers. With an agonized cry, she clutches his shoulders and drags herself to her feet as he rises with her. He clasps her tenderly in his arms.*] My poor pet!

JUDITH. [*frantically clinging to him*]. What shall I do? Oh my God, what shall I do?

ANDERSON. Never mind, never mind, my dearest dear: it was my fault. Come: you're safe now; and you're not hurt, are you? [*He takes his arms from her to see whether she can stand.*] There: that's right, that's right. If only you are not hurt, nothing else matters.

JUDITH. No, no, no: I'm not hurt.

ANDERSON. Thank Heaven for that! Come now: [*leading her to the railed seat and making her sit down beside him*] sit down and rest: you can tell me about it to-morrow. Or, [*misunderstanding her distress*] you shall not tell me at all if it worries you. There, there! [*Cheerfully.*] I'll make you some fresh tea: that will set you up again. [*He goes to the table, and empties the teapot into the slop bowl.*]

JUDITH. [*in a strained tone*]. Tony.

ANDERSON. Yes, dear?

JUDITH. Do you think we are only in a dream now?

ANDERSON. [*glancing round at her for a moment with a pang of anxiety, though he goes on steadily and cheerfully putting fresh tea into the pot*]. Perhaps so, pet. But you may as well dream a cup of tea when you're about it.

JUDITH. Oh, stop, stop. You don't know—[*Distracted she buries her face in her knotted hands.*]

ANDERSON. [*breaking down and coming to her*]. My dear, what is it? I can't bear it any longer: you must tell me. It was all my fault: I was mad to trust him.

JUDITH. No: don't say that. You mustn't say that. He—oh no, no: I can't. Tony: don't speak to me. Take my hands—both my hands. [*He takes them, wondering.*] Make me think of you, not of him. There's danger, frightful danger; but it is your danger; and I can't keep thinking of it: I can't, I can't: my mind goes back to his danger. He must be saved—no: you must be saved: you, you, you. [*She springs up as if to do something or go somewhere, exclaiming*] Oh, Heaven help me!

ANDERSON. [*keeping his seat and holding her hands with resolute composure*]. Calmly, calmly, my pet. You're quite distracted.

JUDITH. I may well be. I don't know what to do. I don't know what to do. [*Tearing her hands away.*] I must save him. [*ANDERSON rises in alarm as she runs wildly to the door. It is opened in her face by ESSIE, who hurries in, full of anxiety. The surprise is so disagreeable to JUDITH that it brings her to her senses. Her tone is sharp and angry as she demands*] What do you want?

ESSIE. I was to come to you.

ANDERSON. Who told you to?

ESSIE. [*staring at him, as if his presence astonished her*]. Are you here?

JUDITH. Of course. Don't be foolish, child.

ANDERSON. Gently, dearest: you'll frighten her. [*Going between them.*] Come here, Essie. [*She comes to him.*] Who sent you?

ESSIE. Dick. He sent me word by a soldier. I was to come here at once and do whatever Mrs. Anderson told me.

ANDERSON. [*enlightened*]. A soldier! Ah, I see it all now! They have arrested Richard. [*JUDITH makes a gesture of despair.*]

ESSIE. No. I asked the soldier. Dick's safe. But the soldier said you had been taken—

ANDERSON. I! [*Bewildered, he turns to JUDITH for an explanation.*]

JUDITH. [*coaxingly*] All right, dear: I understand. [*To ESSIE.*] Thank you, Essie, for coming; but I don't need you now. You may go home.

ESSIE. [*suspicious*] Are you sure Dick has not been touched? Perhaps he told the soldier to say it was the minister. [*Anxiously.*] Mrs. Anderson: do you think it can have been that?

ANDERSON. Tell her the truth if it is so, Judith. She will learn it from the first neighbor she meets in the street. [*JUDITH turns away and covers her eyes with her hands.*]

ESSIE. [*wailing*]. But what will they do to him? Oh, what will they do to him? Will they hang him? [*JUDITH shudders convulsively, and throws herself into the chair in which RICHARD sat at the tea table.*]

ANDERSON. [*patting ESSIE's shoulder and trying to comfort her*]. I hope not. I hope not. Perhaps if you're very quiet and patient, we may be able to help him in some way.

ESSIE. Yes—help him—yes, yes, yes. I'll be good.

ANDERSON. I must go to him at once, Judith.

JUDITH. [*springing up*]. Oh no. You must go away—far away, to some place of safety.

ANDERSON. Pooh!

JUDITH. [*passionately*]. Do you want to kill me? Do you think I can bear to live for days and days with every knock at the door—every footstep—giving me a spasm of terror? to lie awake for nights and nights in an agony of dread, listening for them to come and arrest you?

ANDERSON. Do you think it would be better to know that I had run away from my post at the first sign of danger?

JUDITH. [*bitterly*]. Oh, you won't go. I know it. You'll stay; and I shall go mad.

ANDERSON. My dear, your duty—

JUDITH. [*fiercely*]. What do I care about my duty?

ANDERSON. [shocked]. Judith!

JUDITH. I am doing my duty. I am clinging to my duty. My duty is to get you away, to save you, to leave him to his fate. [Essie utters a cry of distress and sinks on the chair at the fire, sobbing silently.] My instinct is the same as hers—to save him above all things, though it would be so much better for him to die! so much greater! But I know you will take your own way as he took it. I have no power. [She sits down sullenly on the railed seat.] I'm only a woman: I can do nothing but sit here and suffer. Only, tell him I tried to save you—that I did my best to save you.

ANDERSON. My dear, I am afraid he will be thinking more of his own danger than of mine.

JUDITH. Stop; or I shall hate you.

ANDERSON. [*remonstrating*]. Come, am I to leave you if you talk like this! your senses. [*He turns to ESSIE.*] Essie.

ESSIE. [*eagerly rising and drying her eyes*]. Yes?

ANDERSON. Just wait outside a moment, like a good girl: Mrs. Anderson is not well. [*ESSIE looks doubtful.*] Never fear: I'll come to you presently; and I'll go to Dick.

ESSIE. You are sure you will go to him? [*Whispering.*] You won't let her prevent you?

ANDERSON. [*smiling*]. No, no: it's all right. All right. [*She goes.*] That's a good girl. [*He closes the door, and returns to JUDITH.*]

JUDITH. [*seated—rigid*]. You are going to your death.

ANDERSON. [*quaintly*]. Then I shall go in my best coat, dear. [*He turns to the press, beginning to take off his coat.*] Where—? [*He stares at the empty nail for a moment; then looks quickly round to the fire; strides across to it; and lifts RICHARD's coat.*] Why, my dear, it seems that he has gone in my best coat.

JUDITH. [*still motionless*]. Yes.

ANDERSON. Did the soldiers make a mistake?

JUDITH. Yes: they made a mistake.

ANDERSON. He might have told them. Poor fellow, he was too upset, I suppose.

JUDITH. Yes: he might have told them. So might I.

ANDERSON. Well, it's all very puzzling—almost funny. It's curious how these little things strike us even in the most— [*he breaks of and begins putting on RICHARD's coat*] I'd better take him his own coat. I know what he'll say— [*imitating RICHARD's sardonic manner*] "Anxious about my soul, Pastor, and also about your best coat." Eh?

JUDITH. Yes, that is just what he will say to you. [*Vacantly.*] It doesn't matter: I shall never see either of you again.

ANDERSON. [*rallying her*]. Oh pooh, pooh, pooh! [*He sits down beside her.*] Is this how you keep your promise that I shan't be ashamed of my brave wife?

JUDITH. No: this is how I break it. I cannot keep my promises to him: why should I keep my promises to you?

ANDERSON. Don't speak so strangely, my love. It sounds insincere to me. [*She looks unutterable reproach at him.*] Yes, dear, nonsense is always insincere; and my dearest is talking nonsense. Just nonsense. [*Her face darkens into dumb obstinacy. She stares straight before her, and does not look at him again, absorbed in RICHARD's fate. He scans her face; sees that his rallying has produced no effect; and gives it up, making no further effort to conceal his anxiety.*] I wish I knew what has frightened you so. Was there a struggle? Did he fight?

JUDITH. No. He smiled.

ANDERSON. Did he realise his danger, do you think?

JUDITH. He realised yours.

ANDERSON. Mine!

JUDITH. [*monotonously*]. He said, "See that you get him safely out of harm's way." I promised: I can't keep my promise. He said, "Don't for your life let him know of my danger." I've told you of it. He said that if you found it out, you could not save him—that they will hang him and not spare you.

ANDERSON. [*rising in generous indignation*]. And you think that I will let a man with that much good in him die like a dog, when a few words might make him die like a Christian? I'm ashamed of you, Judith.

JUDITH. He will be steadfast in his religion as you are in yours; and you may depend on him to the death. He said so.

ANDERSON. God forgive him! What else did he say?

JUDITH. He said goodbye.

ANDERSON. [*fidgeting nervously to and fro in great concern*]. Poor fellow, poor fellow! You said goodbye to him in all kindness and charity, Judith, I hope.

JUDITH. I kissed him.

ANDERSON. What! Judith!

JUDITH. Are you angry?

ANDERSON. No, no. You were right: you were right. Poor fellow, poor fellow! [*Greatly distressed.*] To be hanged like that at his age! And then did they take him away?

JUDITH. [*wearily*]. Then you were here: that's the next thing I remember. I suppose I fainted. Now bid me goodbye, Tony. Perhaps I shall faint again. I wish I could die.

ANDERSON. No, no, my dear: you must pull yourself together and be sensible. I am in no danger—not the least in the world.

JUDITH. [*solemnly*]. You are going to your death, Tony—your sure death, if God will let innocent men be murdered. They will not let you see him: they will arrest you the moment you give your name. It was for you the soldiers came.

ANDERSON. [*thunderstruck*]. For me!!! [*His fists clinch; his neck thickens; his face reddens; the fleshy purses under his eyes become injected with hot blood; the man of peace vanishes, transfigured into a choleric and formidable man of war. Still, she does not come out of her absorption to look at him: her eyes are steadfast with a mechanical reflection of RICHARD's stead- fastness.*]

JUDITH. He took your place: he is dying to save you. That is why he went in your coat. That is why I kissed him.

ANDERSON. [*exploding*]. Blood an' owns! [*His voice is rough and dominant, his gesture full of brute energy.*] Here! Essie, Essie!

ESSIE. [*running in*]. Yes.

ANDERSON. [*impetuously*]. Off with you as hard as you can run, to the inn. Tell them to saddle the fastest and strongest horse they have [*JUDITH rises breathless, and stares at him incredulously*]—the chestnut mare, if she's fresh—without a moment's delay. Go into the stable yard and tell the black man there that I'll give him a silver dollar if the horse is waiting for me when I come, and that I am close on your heels. Away with you. [*His energy sends ESSIE flying from the room. He pounces on his riding boots; rushes with them to the chair at the fire; and begins pulling them on.*]

JUDITH. [*unable to believe such a thing of him*]. You are not going to him!

ANDERSON. [*busy with the boots*]. Going to him! What good would that do? [*Growling to himself as he gets the first boot on with a wrench*] I'll go to them, so I will. [*To JUDITH peremptorily*] Get me the pistols: I want them. And money, money: I want money—all the money in the house. [*He stoops over the other boot, grumbling*] A great satisfaction it would be to him to have my company on the gallows. [*He pulls on the boot.*]

JUDITH. You are deserting him, then?

ANDERSON. Hold your tongue, woman; and get me the pistols. [*She goes to the press and takes from it a leather belt with two pistols, a powder horn, and a bag of bullets attached to it. She throws it on the table. Then she unlocks a drawer in the press and takes out a purse. ANDERSON grabs the belt and buckles it on, saying*] If they took him for me in my coat, perhaps they'll take me for him in his. [*Hitching the belt into its place*] Do I look like him?

JUDITH. [*turning with the purse in her hand*]. Horribly unlike him.

ANDERSON. [*snatching the purse from her and emptying it on the table*]. Hm! We shall see.

JUDITH. [*sitting down helplessly*]. Is it of any use to pray, do you think, Tony?

ANDERSON. [*counting the money*]. Pray! Can we pray Swindon's rope off Richard's neck?

JUDITH. God may soften Major Swindon's heart.

ANDERSON. [*contemptuously—pocketing a handful of money*]. Let him, then. I am not God; and I must go to work another way. [*JUDITH gasps at the blasphemy. He throws the purse on the table.*] Keep that. I've taken 25 dollars.

JUDITH. Have you forgotten even that you are a minister?

ANDERSON. Minister be—faugh! My hat: where's my hat? [*He snatches up hat and cloak, and puts both on in hot haste.*] Now listen, you. If you can get a word with him by pretending you're his wife, tell him to hold his tongue until morning: that will give me all the start I need.

JUDITH. [*solemnly*]. You may depend on him to the death.

ANDERSON. You're a fool, a fool, Judith [*for a moment checking the torrent of his haste, and speaking with something of his old quiet and impressive conviction*]. You don't know the man you're married to. [*ESSIE returns. He swoops at her at once.*] Well: is the horse ready?

ESSIE. [*breathless*]. It will be ready when you come.

ANDERSON. Good. [*He makes for the door.*]

JUDITH. [*rising and stretching out her arms after him involuntarily*]. Won't you say goodbye?

ANDERSON. And waste another half minute! Psha! [*He rushes out like an avalanche.*]

ESSIE. [*hurrying to JUDITH*]. He has gone to save Richard, hasn't he?

JUDITH. To save Richard! No: Richard has saved him. He has gone to save himself. Richard must die.

ESSIE screams with terror and falls on her knees, hiding her face. JUDITH, without heeding her, looks rigidly straight in front of her, at the vision of RICHARD, dying.

ACT III

Early next morning the sergeant, at the British headquarters in the Town Hall, unlocks the door of a little empty panelled waiting room, and invites Judith to enter. She has had a bad night, probably a rather delirious one; for even in the reality of the raw morning, her fixed gaze comes back at moments when her attention is not strongly held.

The sergeant considers that her feelings do her credit, and is sympathetic in an encouraging military way. Being a fine figure of a man, vain of his uniform and of his rank, he feels specially qualified, in a respectful way, to console her.

SERGEANT. You can have a quiet word with him here, mum.

JUDITH. Shall I have long to wait?

SERGEANT. No, mum, not a minute. We kep him in the Bridewell for the night; and he's just been brought over here for the court martial. Don't fret, mum: he slep like a child, and has made a rare good breakfast.

JUDITH. [*incredulously*]. He is in good spirits!

SERGEANT. Tip top, mum. The chaplain looked in to see him last night; and he won seventeen shillings off him at spoil five. He spent it among us like the gentleman he is. Duty's duty, mum, of course; but you're among friends here. [*The tramp of a couple of soldiers is heard approaching.*] There: I think he's coming. [*RICHARD comes in, without a sign of care or captivity in his bearing. The sergeant nods to the two soldiers, and shows them the key of the room in his hand. They withdraw.*] Your good lady, sir.

RICHARD. [*going to her*]. What! My wife. My adored one. [*He takes her hand and kisses it with a perverse, raffish gallantry.*] How long do you allow a brokenhearted husband for leave-taking, Sergeant?

SERGEANT. As long as we can, sir. We shall not disturb you till the court sits.

RICHARD. But it has struck the hour.

SERGEANT. So it has, sir; but there's a delay. General Burgoyne's just arrived—Gentlemanly Johnny we call him, sir—and he won't have done finding fault with everything this side of half past. I know him, sir: I served with him in Portugal. You may count on twenty minutes, sir; and by your leave I won't waste any more of them. [*He goes out, locking the door. RICHARD immediately drops his raffish manner and turns to JUDITH with considerate sincerity.*]

RICHARD. Mrs. Anderson: this visit is very kind of you. And how are you after last night? I had to leave you before you recovered; but I sent word to Essie to go and look after you. Did she understand the message?

JUDITH. [*breathless and urgent*]. Oh, don't think of me: I haven't come here to talk about myself. Are they going to—to—[*meaning "to hang you"*]?

RICHARD. [*whimsically*]. At noon, punctually. At least, that was when they disposed of Uncle Peter. [*She shudders.*] Is your husband safe? Is he on the wing?

JUDITH. He is no longer my husband.

RICHARD. [*opening his eyes wide*]. Eh?

JUDITH. I disobeyed you. I told him everything. I expected him to come here and save you. I wanted him to come here and save you. He ran away instead.

RICHARD. Well, that's what I meant him to do. What good would his staying have done? They'd only have hanged us both.

JUDITH. [*with reproachful earnestness*]. Richard Dudgeon: on your honour, what would you have done in his place?

RICHARD. Exactly what he has done, of course.

JUDITH. Oh, why will you not be simple with me—honest and straightforward? If you are so selfish as that, why did you let them take you last night?

RICHARD. [*gaily*]. Upon my life, Mrs. Anderson, I don't know. I've been asking myself that question ever since; and I can find no manner of reason for acting as I did.

JUDITH. You know you did it for his sake, believing he was a more worthy man than yourself.

RICHARD. [*laughing*]. Oho! No: that's a very pretty reason, I must say; but I'm not so modest as that. No: it wasn't for his sake.

JUDITH. [*after a pause, during which she looks shamefacedly at him, blushing painfully*]. Was it for my sake?

RICHARD. [*gallantly*]. Well, you had a hand in it. It must have been a little for your sake. You let them take me, at all events.

JUDITH. Oh, do you think I have not been telling myself that all night? Your death will be at my door. [*Impulsively, she gives him her hand, and adds, with intense earnestness*] If I could save you as you saved him, I would do it, no matter how cruel the death was.

RICHARD. [*holding her hand and smiling, but keeping her almost at arm's length*]. I am very sure I shouldn't let you.

JUDITH. Don't you see that I can save you?

RICHARD. How? By changing clothes with me, eh?

JUDITH. [*disengaging her hand to touch his lips with it*]. Don't [*meaning "Don't jest"*]. No: by telling the Court who you really are.

RICHARD. [*frowning*]. No use: they wouldn't spare me; and it would spoil half of his chance of escaping. They are determined to cow us by making an example of somebody on that gallows to-day. Well, let us cow them by showing that we can stand by one another to the death. That is the only force that can send Burgoyne back across the Atlantic and make America a nation.

JUDITH. [*impatiently*]. Oh, what does all that matter?

RICHARD. [*laughing*]. True: what does it matter? what does anything matter? You see, men have these strange notions, Mrs. Anderson; and women see the folly of them.

JUDITH. Women have to lose those they love through them.

RICHARD. They can easily get fresh lovers.

JUDITH. [*revolted*]. Oh! [*Vehemently*] Do you realise that you are going to kill yourself?

RICHARD. The only man I have any right to kill, Mrs. Anderson. Don't be concerned: no woman will lose her lover through my death. [*Smiling*] Bless you, nobody cares for me. Have you heard that my mother is dead?

JUDITH. Dead!

RICHARD. Of heart disease—in the night. Her last word to me was her curse: I don't think I could have borne her blessing. My other relatives will not grieve much on my account. Essie will cry for a day or two; but I have provided for her: I made my own will last night.

JUDITH. [*stonily, after a moment's silence*]. And I!

RICHARD. [*surprised*]. You?

JUDITH. Yes, I. Am I not to care at all?

RICHARD. [*gaily and bluntly*]. Not a scrap. Oh, you expressed your feelings towards me very frankly yesterday. What happened may have softened you for the moment; but believe me, Mrs. Anderson, you don't like a bone in my skin or a hair on my head. I shall be as good a riddance at 12 today as I should have been at 12 yesterday.

JUDITH. [*her voice trembling*]. What can I do to show you that you are mistaken?

RICHARD. Don't trouble. I'll give you credit for liking me a little better than you did. All I say is that my death will not break your heart.

JUDITH. [*almost in a whisper*]. How do you know? [*She puts her hands on his shoulders and looks intently at him.*]

RICHARD. [*amazed—divining the truth*]. Mrs. Anderson!!! [*The bell of the town clock strikes the quarter. He collects himself, and removes her hands, saying rather coldly*] Excuse me: they will be here for me presently. It is too late.

JUDITH. It is not too late. Call me as witness: they will never kill you when they know how heroically you have acted.

RICHARD. [*with some scorn*]. Indeed! But if I don't go through with it, where will the heroism be? I shall simply have tricked them; and they'll hang me for that like a dog. Serve me right too!

JUDITH. [*wildly*]. Oh, I believe you *want* to die.

RICHARD. [*obstinately*]. No I don't.

JUDITH. Then why not try to save yourself? I implore you—listen. You said just now that you saved him for my sake—

yes [*clutching him as he recoils with a gesture of denial*] a little for my sake. Well, save yourself for my sake. And I will go with you to the end of the world.

RICHARD. [*taking her by the wrists and holding her a little way from him, looking steadily at her*]. Judith.

JUDITH. [*breathless—delighted at the name*]. Yes.

RICHARD. If I said—to please you—that I did what I did ever so little for your sake, I lied as men always lie to women. You know how much I have lived with worthless men—aye, and worthless women too. Well, they could all rise to some sort of goodness and kindness when they were in love. [*The word love comes from him with true Puritan scorn.*] That has taught me to set very little store by the goodness that only comes out red hot. What I did last night, I did in cold blood, caring not half so much for your husband, or [*ruthlessly*] for you [*she droops, stricken*] as I do for myself. I had no motive and no interest: all I can tell you is that when it came to the point whether I would take my neck out of the noose and put another man's into it, I could not do it. I don't know why not: I see myself as a fool for my pains; but I could not and I cannot. I have been brought up standing by the law of my own nature; and I may not go against it, gallows or no gallows. [*She has slowly raised her head and is now looking full at him.*] I should have done the same for any other man in the town, or any other man's wife. [*Releasing her.*] Do you understand that?

JUDITH. Yes: you mean that you do not love me.

RICHARD. [*revolted—with fierce contempt*]. Is that all it means to you?

JUDITH. What more—what worse—can it mean to me?[*The sergeant knocks. The blow on the door jars on her heart.*] Oh, one moment more. [*She throws herself on her knees.*] I pray to you—

RICHARD. Hush! [*Calling*] Come in. [*The sergeant unlocks the door and opens it. The guard is with him.*]

SERGEANT [*coming in*]. Time's up, sir.

RICHARD. Quite ready, Sergeant. Now, my dear. [*He attempts to raise her.*]

JUDITH. [*clinging to him*]. Only one thing more—I entreat, I implore you. Let me be present in the court. I have seen Major Swindon: he said I should be allowed if you asked it. You will ask it. It is my last request: I shall never ask you anything again. [*She clasps his knee.*] I beg and pray it of you.

RICHARD. If I do, will you be silent?

JUDITH. Yes.

RICHARD. You will keep faith?

JUDITH. I will keep—[*She breaks down, sobbing.*]

RICHARD. [*taking her arm to lift her*]. Just—her other arm, Sergeant. *They go out, she sobbing convulsively, supported by the two men.*

Meanwhile, the Council Chamber is ready for the court martial. It is a large, lofty room, with a chair of state in the middle under a tall canopy with a gilt crown, and maroon curtains with the royal monogram G. R. In front of the chair is a table, also draped in maroon, with a bell, a heavy inkstand, and writing materials on it. Several chairs are set at the table. The door is at the right hand of the occupant of the chair of state when it has an occupant: at present it is empty. MAJOR SWINDON, a pale, sandy-haired, very conscientious looking man of about 45, sits at the end of the table with his back to the door, writing. He is alone until the SERGEANT announces the GENERAL in a subdued manner which suggests that GENTLEMANLY JOHNNY has been making his presence felt rather heavily.

SERGEANT. The General, sir.

SWINDON rises hastily. The General comes in, the SERGEANT goes out. GENERAL BURGOYNE is 55, and very well preserved. He is a man of fashion, gallant enough to have made a distinguished marriage by an elopement, witty enough to write successful comedies, aristocratically-connected enough to have had opportunities of high military distinction. His eyes, large, brilliant, apprehensive, and intelligent, are his most remarkable feature: without them his fine nose and small mouth would suggest rather more fastidiousness and less force than go to the making of a first rate general. Just now the eyes are angry and tragic, and the mouth and nostrils tense.

BURGOYNE. Major Swindon, I presume.

SWINDON. Yes. General Burgoyne, if I mistake not. [*They bow to one another ceremoniously.*] I am glad to have the support of your presence this morning. It is not particularly lively business, hanging this poor devil of a minister.

BURGOYNE. [*throwing himself onto SWINDON'S chair*]. No, sir, it is not. It is making too much of the fellow to execute him: what more could you have done if he had been a member of the Church of England? Martyrdom, sir, is what these people like: it is the only way in which a man can become famous without ability. However, you have committed us to hanging him: and the sooner he is hanged the better.

SWINDON. We have arranged it for 12 o'clock. Nothing remains to be done except to try him.

BURGOYNE. [*looking at him with suppressed anger*]. Nothing—except to save our own necks, perhaps. Have you heard the news from Springtown?

SWINDON. Nothing special. The latest reports are satisfactory.

BURGOYNE. [*rising in amazement*]. Satisfactory, sir! Satisfactory!! [*He stares at him for a moment, and then adds, with grim intensity*] I am glad you take that view of them.

SWINDON. [*puzzled*]. Do I understand that in your opinion—-

BURGOYNE. I do not express my opinion. I never stoop to that habit of profane language which unfortunately coarsens our profession. If I did, sir, perhaps I should be able to express my opinion of the news from Springtown—the news which *you* [*severely*] have apparently not heard. How soon do you get news from your supports here?—in the course of a month eh?

SWINDON. [*turning sulky*]. I suppose the reports have been taken to you, sir, instead of to me. Is there anything serious?

BURGOYNE. [*taking a report from his pocket and holding it up*]. Springtown's in the hands of the rebels. [*He throws the report on the table.*]

SWINDON. [*aghast*]. Since yesterday!

BURGOYNE. Since two o'clock this morning. Perhaps WE shall be in their hands before two o'clock to-morrow morning. Have you thought of that?

SWINDON. [*confidently*]. As to that, General, the British soldier will give a good account of himself.

BURGOYNE. [*bitterly*]. And therefore, I suppose, sir, the British officer need not know his business: the British soldier will get him out of all his blunders with the bayonet. In future, sir, I must ask you to be a little less generous with the blood of your men, and a little more generous with your own brains.

SWINDON. I am sorry I cannot pretend to your intellectual eminence, sir. I can only do my best, and rely on the devotion of my countrymen.

BURGOYNE. [*suddenly becoming suavely sarcastic*]. May I ask are you writing a melodrama, Major Swindon?

SWINDON. [*flushing*]. No, sir.

BURGOYNE. What a pity! *What* a pity! [*Dropping his sarcastic tone and facing him suddenly and seriously*] Do you at all realize, sir, that we have nothing standing between us and destruction but our own bluff and the sheepishness of these colonists? They are men of the same English stock as ourselves: six to one of us [*repeating it emphatically*], six to one, sir; and nearly half our troops are Hessians, Brunswickers, German dragoons, and Indians with scalping knives. These are the countrymen on whose devotion you rely! Suppose the colonists find a leader! Suppose the news from Springtown should turn out to mean that they have already found a leader! What shall we do then? Eh?

SWINDON. [*sullenly*]. Our duty, sir, I presume.

BURGOYNE. [*again sarcastic—giving him up as a fool*]. Quite so, quite so. Thank you, Major Swindon, thank you. Now you've settled the question, sir—thrown a flood of light on the situation. What a comfort to me to feel that I have at my side so devoted and able an officer to support me in this emergency! I think, sir, it will probably relieve both our feelings if we proceed to hang this dissenter without further delay [*he strikes the bell*], especially as I am debarred by my principles from the customary military vent for my feelings. [*The SERGEANT appears.*] Bring your man in.

SERGEANT. Yes, sir.

BURGOYNE. And mention to any officer you may meet that the court cannot wait any longer for him.

SWINDON. [*keeping his temper with difficulty*]. The staff is perfectly ready, sir. They have been waiting your convenience for fully half an hour. *perfectly* ready, sir.

BURGOYNE. [*blandly*]. So am I. [*Several officers come in and take their seats. One of them sits at the end of the table furthest from the door, and acts throughout as clerk to the court, making notes of the proceedings. The uniforms are those of the 9th, 20th, 21st, 24th, 47th, 53rd, and 62nd British Infantry. One officer is a Major General of the Royal Artillery. There are also German officers of the Hessian Rifles, and of German dragoon and Brunswicker regiments.*] Oh, good morning, gentlemen. Sorry to disturb you, I am sure. Very good of you to spare us a few moments.

SWINDON. Will you preside, sir?

BURGOYNE. [*becoming additionally, polished, lofty, sarcastic and urbane now that he is in public*]. No, sir: I feel my own deficiencies too keenly to presume so far. If you will kindly allow me, I will sit at the feet of Gamaliel. [*He takes the chair at the end of the table next the door, and motions SWINDON to the chair of state, waiting for him to be seated before sitting himself.*]

SWINDON. [*greatly annoyed*]. As you please, sir. I am only trying to do my duty under excessively trying circumstances. [*He takes his place in the chair of state.*]

BURGOYNE, relaxing his studied demeanor for the moment, sits down and begins to read the report with knitted brows and careworn looks, reflecting on his desperate situation and SWINDON'S uselessness. RICHARD is brought in. JUDITH walks beside him. Two soldiers precede and two follow him, with the SERGEANT in command. They cross the room to the wall opposite the door; but when RICHARD has just passed before the chair of state the SERGEANT stops

him with a touch on the arm, and posts himself behind him,
at his elbow. JUDITH stands timidly at the wall. The four
soldiers place themselves in a squad near her.

BURGOYNE. [*looking up and seeing JUDITH*]. Who is that
woman?

SERGEANT. Prisoner's wife, sir.

SWINDON. [*nervously*]. She begged me to allow her to be
present; and I thought—

BURGOYNE. [*completing the sentence for him ironically*]. You
thought it would be a pleasure for her. Quite so, quite so.
[*Blandly*] Give the lady a chair; and make her thoroughly
comfortable.

The SERGEANT fetches a chair and places it near
RICHARD.

JUDITH. Thank you, sir. [*She sits down after an awe-stricken*
curtsy to BURGOYNE, which he acknowledges by a
dignified bend of his head.]

SWINDON. [*to RICHARD, sharply*]. Your name, sir?

RICHARD. [*affable, but obstinate*]. Come: you don't mean to
say that you've brought me here without knowing who I am?

SWINDON. As a matter of form, sir, give your name.

RICHARD. As a matter of form then, my name is Anthony
Anderson, Presbyterian minister in this town.

BURGOYNE. [*interested*]. Indeed! Pray, Mr. Anderson, what do
you gentlemen believe?

RICHARD. I shall be happy to explain if time is allowed me. I
cannot undertake to complete your conversion in less than a
fortnight.

SWINDON. [*snubbing him*]. We are not here to discuss your
views.

BURGOYNE. [*with an elaborate bow to the unfortunate*
SWINDON]. I stand rebuked.

SWINDON. [*embarrassed*]. Oh, not you, I as—

BURGOYNE. Don't mention it. [*To RICHARD, very politely*]
Any political views, Mr. Anderson?

RICHARD. I understand that that is just what we are here to find
out.

SWINDON. [*severely*]. Do you mean to deny that you are a rebel?

RICHARD. I am an American, sir.

SWINDON. What do you expect me to think of that speech, Mr. Anderson?

RICHARD. I never expect a soldier to think, sir.

BURGOYNE is boundlessly delighted by this retort, which almost reconciles him to the loss of America.

SWINDON. [*whitening with anger*]. I advise you not to be insolent, prisoner.

RICHARD. You can't help yourself, General. When you make up your mind to hang a man, you put yourself at a disadvantage with him. Why should I be civil to you? I may as well be hanged for a sheep as a lamb.

SWINDON. You have no right to assume that the court has made up its mind without a fair trial. And you will please not address me as General. I am Major Swindon.

RICHARD. A thousand pardons. I thought I had the honor of addressing Gentlemanly Johnny.

Sensation among the officers. The sergeant has a narrow escape from a guffaw.

BURGOYNE. [*with extreme suavity*]. I believe I am Gentlemanly Johnny, sir, at your service. My more intimate friends call me General Burgoyne. [*RICHARD bows with perfect politeness.*] You will understand, sir, I hope, since you seem to be a gentleman and a man of some spirit in spite of your calling, that if we should have the misfortune to hang you, we shall do so as a mere matter of political necessity and military duty, without any personal ill-feeling.

RICHARD. Oh, quite so. That makes all the difference in the world, of course.

They all smile in spite of themselves: and some of the younger officers burst out laughing.

JUDITH. [*her dread and horror deepening at every one of these jests and compliments*]. How *can* you?

RICHARD. You promised to be silent.

BURGOYNE. [*to JUDITH, with studied courtesy*]. Believe me, madam, your husband is placing us under the greatest obligation by taking this very disagreeable business so thoroughly in the spirit of a gentleman. Sergeant: give Mr. Anderson a chair. [*The sergeant does so. RICHARD sits down.*] Now, Major Swindon: we are waiting for you.

SWINDON. You are aware, I presume, Mr. Anderson, of your obligations as a subject of His Majesty King George the Third.

RICHARD. I am aware, sir, that His Majesty King George the Third is about to hang me because I object to Lord North's robbing me.

SWINDON. That is a treasonable speech, sir.

RICHARD. [*briefly*]. Yes. I meant it to be.

BURGOYNE. [*strongly deprecating this line of defence, but still polite*]. Don't you think, Mr. Anderson, that this is rather—if you will excuse the word—a vulgar line to take? Why should you cry out robbery because of a stamp duty and a tea duty and so forth? After all, it is the essence of your position as a gentleman that you pay with a good grace.

RICHARD. It is not the money, General. But to be swindled by a pig-headed lunatic like King George.

SWINDON. [*scandalised*]. Chut, sir—silence!

SERGEANT [*in stentorian tones, greatly shocked*]. Silence!

BURGOYNE. [*unruffled*]. Ah, that is another point of view. My position does not allow of my going into that, except in private. But [*shrugging his shoulders*] of course, Mr. Anderson, if you are determined to be hanged [*JUDITH flinches*], there's nothing more to be said. An unusual taste! however [*with a final shrug*]—!

SWINDON. [*to BURGOYNE*]. Shall we call witnesses?

RICHARD. What need is there of witnesses? If the townspeople here had listened to me, you would have found the streets barricaded, the houses loopholed, and the people in arms to hold the town against you to the last man. But you arrived, unfortunately, before we had got out of the talking stage; and then it was too late.

SWINDON. [*severely*]. Well, sir, we shall teach you and your townspeople a lesson they will not forget. Have you anything more to say?

RICHARD. I think you might have the decency to treat me as a prisoner of war, and shoot me like a man instead of hanging me like a dog.

BURGOYNE. [*sympathetically*]. Now there, Mr. Anderson, you talk like a civilian, if you will excuse my saying so. Have you any idea of the average marksmanship of the army of His Majesty King George the Third? If we make you up a firing party, what will happen? Half of them will miss you: the rest will make a mess of the business and leave you to the provo-marshal's pistol. Whereas we can hang you in a perfectly workmanlike and agreeable way. [*Kindly*] Let me persuade you to be hanged, Mr. Anderson?

JUDITH. [*sick with horror*]. My God!

RICHARD. [*to JUDITH*]. Your promise! [*To BURGOYNE*] Thank you, General: that view of the case did not occur to me before. To oblige you, I withdraw my objection to the rope. Hang me, by all means.

BURGOYNE. [*smoothly*]. Will 12 o'clock suit you, Mr. Anderson?

RICHARD. I shall be at your disposal then, General.

BURGOYNE. [*rising*]. Nothing more to be said, gentlemen. [*They all rise.*]

JUDITH. [*rushing to the table*]. Oh, you are not going to murder a man like that, without a proper trial—without thinking of what you are doing—without—[*She cannot find words.*]

RICHARD. Is this how you keep your promise?

JUDITH. If I am not to speak, you must. Defend yourself: save yourself: tell them the truth.

RICHARD. [*worriedly*]. I have told them truth enough to hang me ten times over. If you say another word you will risk other lives; but you will not save mine.

BURGOYNE. My good lady, our only desire is to save unpleasantness. What satisfaction would it give you to have a solemn fuss made, with my friend Swindon in a black cap and so forth? I am sure we are greatly indebted to the admirable tact and gentlemanly feeling shown by your husband.

JUDITH. [*throwing the words in his face*]. Oh, you are mad. Is it nothing to you what wicked thing you do if only you do it like a gentleman? Is it nothing to you whether you are a murderer or not, if only you murder in a red coat? [*Desperately*] You shall not hang him: that man is not my husband.

The officers look at one another, and whisper: some of the Germans asking their neighbors to explain what the woman has said. BURGOYNE, who has been visibly shaken by JUDITH'S reproach, recovers himself promptly at this new development. RICHARD meanwhile raises his voice above the buzz.

RICHARD. I appeal to you, gentlemen, to put an end to this. She will not believe that she cannot save me. Break up the court.

BURGOYNE. [*in a voice so quiet and firm that it restores silence at once*]. One moment, Mr. Anderson. One moment, gentlemen. [*He resumes his seat. SWINDON and the officers follow his example.*] Let me understand you clearly, madam. Do you mean that this gentleman is not your husband, or merely—I wish to put this with all delicacy—that you are not his wife?

JUDITH. I don't know what you mean. I say that he is not my husband—that my husband has escaped. This man took his place to save him. Ask anyone in the town—send out into the street for the first person you find there, and bring him in as a witness. He will tell you that the prisoner is not Anthony Anderson.

BURGOYNE. [*quietly, as before*]. Sergeant.

SERGEANT. Yes sir.

BURGOYNE. Go out into the street and bring in the first townsman you see there.

SERGEANT [*making for the door*]. Yes sir.

BURGOYNE. [*as the sergeant passes*]. The first clean, sober townsman you see.

SERGEANT. Yes Sir. [*He goes out.*]

BURGOYNE. Sit down, Mr. Anderson—if I may call you so for the present. [*RICHARD sits down.*] Sit down, madam, whilst we wait. Give the lady a newspaper.

RICHARD. [*indignantly*]. Shame!

BURGOYNE. [*keenly, with a half smile*]. If you are not her husband, sir, the case is not a serious one—for her. [*RICHARD bites his lip silenced.*]

JUDITH. [*to RICHARD, as she returns to her seat*]. I couldn't help it. [*He shakes his head. She sits down.*]

BURGOYNE. You will understand of course, Mr. Anderson, that you must not build on this little incident. We are bound to make an example of somebody.

RICHARD. I quite understand. I suppose there's no use in my explaining.

BURGOYNE. I think we should prefer independent testimony, if you don't mind.

The SERGEANT, with a packet of papers in his hand, returns conducting CHRISTY, who is much scared.

SERGEANT [*giving BURGOYNE the packet*]. Dispatches, Sir. Delivered by a corporal of the 53rd. Dead beat with hard riding, sir.

BURGOYNE opens the dispatches, and presently becomes absorbed in them. They are so serious as to take his attention completely from the court martial.

SERGEANT [*to CHRISTY*]. Now then. Attention; and take your hat off. [*He posts himself in charge of CHRISTY, who stands on BURGOYNE's side of the court.*]

RICHARD. [*in his usual bullying tone to CHRISTY*]. Don't be frightened, you fool: you're only wanted as a witness. They're not going to hang *you*.

SWINDON. What's your name?

CHRISTY. Christy.

RICHARD. [*impatiently*]. Christopher Dudgeon, you blatant idiot. Give your full name.

SWINDON. Be silent, prisoner. You must not prompt the witness.

RICHARD. Very well. But I warn you you'll get nothing out of him unless you shake it out of him. He has been too well brought up by a pious mother to have any sense or manhood left in him.

BURGOYNE. [*springing up and speaking to the sergeant in a startling voice*]. Where is the man who brought these?

SERGEANT. In the guard-room, sir.

BURGOYNE goes out with a haste that sets the officers exchanging looks.

SWINDON. [*to CHRISTY*]. Do you know Anthony Anderson, the Presbyterian minister?

CHRISTY. Of course I do. [*Implying that SWINDON must be an ass not to know it.*]

SWINDON. Is he here?

CHRISTY. [*staring round*]. I don't know.

SWINDON. Do you see him?

CHRISTY. No.

SWINDON. You seem to know the prisoner?

CHRISTY. Do you mean Dick?

SWINDON. Which is Dick?

CHRISTY. [*pointing to RICHARD*]. Him.

SWINDON. What is his name?

CHRISTY. Dick.

RICHARD. Answer properly, you jumping jackass. What do they know about Dick?

CHRISTY. Well, you are Dick, ain't you? What am I to say?

SWINDON. Address me, sir; and do you, prisoner, be silent. Tell us who the prisoner is.

CHRISTY. He's my brother Dudgeon.

SWINDON. Your brother!

CHRISTY. Yes.

SWINDON. You are sure he is not Anderson.

CHRISTY. Who?

RICHARD. [*exasperatedly*]. Me, me, me, you—

SWINDON. Silence, sir.

SERGEANT [*shouting*]. Silence.

RICHARD. [*impatiently*]. Yah! [*To CHRISTY*] He wants to know am I Minister Anderson. Tell him, and stop grinning like a zany.

CHRISTY. [*grinning more than ever*]. *You* Pastor Anderson! [*To SWINDON*] Why, Mr. Anderson's a minister—a very good man; and Dick's a bad character: the respectable people won't speak to him. He's the bad brother: I'm the good one, [*The officers laugh outright. The soldiers grin.*]

SWINDON. Who arrested this man?

SERGEANT. I did, sir. I found him in the minister's house, sitting at tea with the lady with his coat off, quite at home. If he isn't married to her, he ought to be.

SWINDON. Did he answer to the minister's name?

SERGEANT. Yes sir, but not to a minister's nature. You ask the chaplain, sir.

SWINDON. [*to RICHARD, threateningly*]. So, sir, you have attempted to cheat us. And your name is Richard Dudgeon?

RICHARD. You've found it out at last, have you?

SWINDON. Dudgeon is a name well known to us, eh?

RICHARD. Yes: Peter Dudgeon, whom you murdered, was my uncle.

SWINDON. Hm! [*He compresses his lips and looks at RICHARD with vindictive gravity.*]

CHRISTY. Are they going to hang you, Dick?

RICHARD. Yes. Get out: they've done with you.

CHRISTY. And I may keep the china peacocks?

RICHARD. [*jumping up*]. Get out. Get out, you blithering baboon, you. [*CHRISTY flies, panicstricken.*]

SWINDON. [*rising—all rise*]. Since you have taken the minister's place, Richard Dudgeon, you shall go through with it. The execution will take place at 12 o'clock as arranged; and unless Anderson surrenders before then you shall take his place on the gallows. Sergeant: take your man out.

JUDITH. [*distracted*]. No, no—

SWINDON. [*fiercely, dreading a renewal of her entreaties*]. Take that woman away.

RICHARD. [*springing across the table with a tiger-like bound, and seizing SWINDON by the throat*]. You infernal scoundrel.

The SERGEANT rushes to the rescue from one side, the soldiers from the other. They seize RICHARD and drag him back to his place. SWINDON, who has been thrown supine on the table, rises, arranging his stock. He is about to speak, when he is anticipated by BURGOYNE, who has just appeared at the door with two papers in his hand: a white letter and a blue dispatch.

BURGOYNE. [*advancing to the table, elaborately cool*]. What is this? What's happening? Mr. Anderson: I'm astonished at you.

RICHARD. I am sorry I disturbed you, General. I merely wanted to strangle your understrapper there. [*Breaking out violently at SWINDON*] Why do you raise the devil in me by bullying the woman like that? You oatmeal faced dog, I'd twist your cursed head off with the greatest satisfaction. [*He puts out his hands to the sergeant*] Here: handcuff me, will you; or I'll not undertake to keep my fingers off him.

The SERGEANT takes out a pair of handcuffs and looks to BURGOYNE for instructions.

BURGOYNE. Have you addressed profane language to the lady, Major Swindon?

SWINDON. [*very angry*]. No, sir, certainly not. That question should not have been put to me. I ordered the woman to be removed, as she was disorderly; and the fellow sprang at me. Put away those handcuffs. I am perfectly able to take care of myself.

RICHARD. Now you talk like a man, I have no quarrel with you.

BURGOYNE. Mr. Anderson—

SWINDON. His name is Dudgeon, sir, Richard Dudgeon. He is an impostor.

BURGOYNE. [*brusquely*]. Nonsense, sir; you hanged Dudgeon at Springtown.

RICHARD. It was my uncle, General.

BURGOYNE. Oh, your uncle. [*To SWINDON, handsomely*] I beg your pardon, Major Swindon. [*SWINDON acknowledges the apology stiffly. BURGOYNE turns to RICHARD*] We are somewhat unfortunate in our relations with your family. Well, Mr. Dudgeon, what I wanted to ask you is this: Who is [*reading the name from the letter*] William Maindeck Parshotter?

RICHARD. He is the Mayor of Springtown.

BURGOYNE. Is William—Maindeck and so on—a man of his word?

RICHARD. Is he selling you anything?

BURGOYNE. No.

RICHARD. Then you may depend on him.

BURGOYNE. Thank you, Mr.—'m Dudgeon. By the way, since you are not Mr. Anderson, do we still—eh, Major Swindon? [*meaning "do we still hang him?"*]

RICHARD. The arrangements are unaltered, General.

BURGOYNE. Ah, indeed. I am sorry. Good morning, Mr. Dudgeon. Good morning, madam.

RICHARD. [*interrupting JUDITH almost fiercely as she is about to make some wild appeal, and taking her arm resolutely*]. Not one word more. Come.

She looks imploringly at him, but is overborne by his determination. They are marched out by the four soldiers: the SERGEANT, very sulky, walking between SWINDON and RICHARD, whom he watches as if he were a dangerous animal.

BURGOYNE. Gentlemen: we need not detain you. Major Swindon: a word with you. [*The officers go out. BURGOYNE waits with unruffled serenity until the last of them disappears. Then he becomes very grave, and addresses SWINDON for the first time without his title.*] Swindon: do you know what this is [*showing him the letter*]?

SWINDON. What?

BURGOYNE. A demand for a safe-conduct for an officer of their militia to come here and arrange terms with us.

SWINDON. Oh, they are giving in.

BURGOYNE. They add that they are sending the man who raised Springtown last night and drove us out; so that we may know that we are dealing with an officer of importance.

SWINDON. Pooh!

BURGOYNE. He will be fully empowered to arrange the terms of—guess what.

SWINDON. Their surrender, I hope.

BURGOYNE. No: our evacuation of the town. They offer us just six hours to clear out.

SWINDON. What monstrous impudence!

BURGOYNE. What shall we do, eh?

SWINDON. March on Springtown and strike a decisive blow at once.

BURGOYNE. [*quietly*]. Hm! [*Turning to the door*] Come to the adjutant's office.

SWINDON. What for?

BURGOYNE. To write out that safe-conduct. [*He puts his hand to the door knob to open it.*]

SWINDON. [*who has not budged*]. General Burgoyne.

BURGOYNE. [*returning*]. Sir?

SWINDON. It is my duty to tell you, sir, that I do not consider the threats of a mob of rebellious tradesmen a sufficient reason for our giving way.

BURGOYNE. [*imperturbable*]. Suppose I resign my command to you, what will you do?

SWINDON. I will undertake to do what we have marched south from Boston to do, and what General Howe has marched north from New York to do: effect a junction at Albany and wipe out the rebel army with our united forces.

BURGOYNE. [*enigmatically*]. And will you wipe out our enemies in London, too?

SWINDON. In London! What enemies?

BURGOYNE. [*forcibly*]. Jobbery and snobbery, incompetence and Red Tape. [*He holds up the dispatch and adds, with despair in his face and voice*] I have just learnt, sir, that General Howe is still in New York.

SWINDON. [*thunderstruck*]. Good God! He has disobeyed orders!

BURGOYNE. [*with sardonic calm*]. He has received no orders, sir. Some gentleman in London forgot to dispatch them: he was leaving town for his holiday, I believe. To avoid upsetting his arrangements, England will lose her American colonies; and in a few days you and I will be at Saratoga with 5,000 men to face 16,000 rebels in an impregnable position.

SWINDON. [*appalled*]. Impossible!

BURGOYNE. [*coldly*]. I beg your pardon!

SWINDON. I can't believe it! What will History say?

BURGOYNE. History, sir, will tell lies, as usual. Come: we must send the safe-conduct. [*He goes out.*]

SWINDON. [*following distractedly*]. My God, my God! We shall be wiped out.

As noon approaches there is excitement in the market place. The gallows which hangs there permanently for the terror of evildoers, with such minor advertizers and examples of crime as the pillory, the whipping post, and the stocks, has a new rope attached, with the noose hitched up to one of the uprights, out of reach of the boys. Its ladder, too, has been brought out and placed in position by the town beadle, who stands by to guard it from unauthorized climbing. The Websterbridge townsfolk are present in force, and in high spirits; for the news has spread that it is the devil's disciple and not the minister that the Continentals [so they call BURGOYNE'S forces] are about to hang: consequently the execution can be enjoyed without any misgiving as to its righteousness, or to the cowardice of allowing it to take place without a struggle. There is even some fear of a disappointment as midday approaches and the arrival of the beadle with the ladder remains the only sign of preparation. But at last reassuring shouts of Here they come: Here they are, are heard; and a company of soldiers with fixed bayonets, half British infantry, half HESSIANS, tramp quickly into the middle of the market place, driving the crowd to the sides.

SERGEANT. Halt. Front. Dress. [*The soldiers change their column into a square enclosing the gallows, their petty officers, energetically led by the sergeant, hustling the persons who find themselves inside the square out at the corners.*] Now then! Out of it with you: out of it. Some o' you'll get strung up yourselves presently. Form that square there, will you, you damned Hoosians. No use talkin' German to them: talk to their toes with the butt ends of your muskets: they'll understand that. *Get* out of it, will you? [*He comes upon JUDITH, standing near the gallows.*] Now then: *you've* no call here.

JUDITH. May I not stay? What harm am I doing?

SERGEANT. I want none of your argufying. You ought to be ashamed of yourself, running to see a man hanged that's not your husband. And he's no better than yourself. I told my major he was a gentleman; and then he goes and tries to strangle him, and calls his blessed Majesty a lunatic. So out of it with you, double quick.

JUDITH. Will you take these two silver dollars and let me stay? *The SERGEANT, without an instant's hesitation, looks quickly and furtively round as he shoots the money dexterously into his pocket. Then he raises his voice in virtuous indignation.*

SERGEANT. *Me* take money in the execution of my duty! Certainly not. Now I'll tell you what I'll do, to teach you to corrupt the King's officer. I'll put you under arrest until the execution's over. You just stand there; and don't let me see you as much as move from that spot until you're let. [*With a swift wink at her he points to the corner of the square behind the gallows on his right, and turns noisily away, shouting*] Now then dress up and keep 'em back, will you?

Cries of Hush and Silence are heard among the townsfolk; and the sound of a military band, playing the Dead March from Saul, is heard. The crowd becomes quiet at once; and the Sergeant and petty officers, hurrying to the back of the square, with a few whispered orders and some stealthy hustling cause it to open and admit the funeral procession, which is protected from the crowd by a double file of soldiers. First come BURGOYNE and SWINDON, who, on entering the square, glance with distaste at the gallows, and avoid passing under it by wheeling a little to the right and stationing themselves on that side. Then MR. BRUDENELL, the chaplain, in his surplice, with his prayer book open in his hand, walking beside RICHARD, who is moody and disorderly. He walks doggedly through the gallows framework, and posts himself a little in front of it. Behind him comes the executioner, a stalwart soldier in his shirtsleeves. Following him, two soldiers haul a light military waggon. Finally comes the band, which posts itself at the back of the square, and finishes the Dead March. JUDITH, watching RICHARD painfully, steals down to the gallows, and stands leaning against its right post. During the conversation which follows, the two soldiers place the cart under the gallows, and stand by the shafts, which point backwards. The executioner takes a set of steps from the cart and places it ready for the prisoner to mount. Then he climbs the tall ladder which stands against the gallows, and cuts the string by which the rope is hitched up; so that the noose drops dangling over the cart, into which he steps as he descends.

RICHARD. [*with suppressed impatience, to BRUDENELL*]. Look here, sir: this is no place for a man of your profession. Hadn't you better go away?

SWINDON. I appeal to you, prisoner, if you have any sense of decency left, to listen to the ministrations of the chaplain, and pay due heed to the solemnity of the occasion.

THE CHAPLAIN. [*gently reproving RICHARD*]. Try to control yourself, and submit to the divine will. [He lifts his book to proceed with the service.]

RICHARD. Answer for your own will, sir, and those of your accomplices here [*indicating BURGOYNE and SWINDON*]: I see little divinity about them or you. You talk to me of Christianity when you are in the act of hanging your enemies. Was there ever such blasphemous nonsense! [*To SWINDON, more rudely*] You've got up the solemnity of the occasion, as you call it, to impress the people with your own dignity—Handel's music and a clergyman to make murder look like piety! Do you suppose I am going to help you? You've asked me to choose the rope because you don't know your own trade well enough to shoot me properly. Well, hang away and have done with it.

SWINDON. [*to the CHAPLAIN*]. Can you do nothing with him, Mr. Brudenell?

CHAPLAIN. I will try, sir. [*Beginning to read*] Man that is born of woman hath—

RICHARD. [*fixing his eyes on him*]. "Thou shalt not kill."
The book drops in BRUDENELL'S hands.

CHAPLAIN. [*confessing his embarrassment*]. What am I to say, Mr. Dudgeon?

RICHARD. Let me alone, man, can't you?

BURGOYNE. [*with extreme urbanity*]. I think, Mr. Brudenell, that as the usual professional observations seem to strike Mr. Dudgeon as incongruous under the circumstances, you had better omit them until—er—until Mr. Dudgeon can no longer be inconvenienced by them. [*BRUDENELL, with a shrug, shuts his book and retires behind the gallows.*] You seem in a hurry, Mr. Dudgeon.

RICHARD. [*with the horror of death upon him*]. Do you think this is a pleasant sort of thing to be kept waiting for? You've made up your mind to commit murder: well, do it and have done with it.

BURGOYNE. Mr. Dudgeon: we are only doing this—

RICHARD. Because you're paid to do it.

SWINDON. You insolent—[*He swallows his rage.*]

BURGOYNE. [*with much charm of manner*]. Ah, I am really sorry that you should think that, Mr. Dudgeon. If you knew what my commission cost me, and what my pay is, you would think better of me. I should be glad to part from you on friendly terms.

RICHARD. Hark ye, General Burgoyne. If you think that I like being hanged, you're mistaken. I don't like it; and I don't mean to pretend that I do. And if you think I'm obliged to you for hanging me in a gentlemanly way, you're wrong there too. I take the whole business in devilish bad part; and the only satisfaction I have in it is that you'll feel a good deal meaner than I'll look when it's over. [*He turns away, and is striding to the cart when JUDITH advances and interposes with her arms stretched out to him. RICHARD, feeling that a very little will upset his self-possession, shrinks from her, crying*] What are you doing here? This is no place for you. [*She makes a gesture as if to touch him. He recoils impatiently.*] No: go away, go away; you'll unnerve me. Take her away, will you?

JUDITH. Won't you bid me good-bye?

RICHARD. [*allowing her to take his hand*]. Oh good-bye, good-bye. Now go—go—quickly. [*She clings to his hand—will not be put off with so cold a last farewell—at last, as he tries to disengage himself, throws herself on his breast in agony.*]

SWINDON. [*angrily to the SERGEANT, who, alarmed at JUDITH's movement, has come from the back of the square to pull her back, and stopped irresolutely on finding that he is too late*]. How is this? Why is she inside the lines?

SERGEANT [*guiltily*]. I dunno, sir. She's that artful can't keep her away.

BURGOYNE. You were bribed.

SERGEANT [*protesting*]. No, Sir—

SWINDON. [*severely*]. Fall back. [*He obeys.*]

RICHARD. [*imploringly to those around him, and finally to BURGOYNE, as the least stolid of them*]. Take her away. Do you think I want a woman near me now?

BURGOYNE. [*going to JUDITH and taking her hand*]. Here, madam: you had better keep inside the lines; but stand here behind us; and don't look.

RICHARD, with a great sobbing sigh of relief as she releases him and turns to BURGOYNE, flies for refuge to the cart and mounts into it. The executioner takes off his coat and pinions him.

JUDITH. [*resisting BURGOYNE quietly and drawing her hand away*]. No: I must stay. I won't look. [*She goes to the right of the gallows. She tries to look at RICHARD, but turns away with a frightful shudder, and falls on her knees in prayer. BRUDENELL comes towards her from the back of the square.*]

BURGOYNE. [*nodding approvingly as she kneels*]. Ah, quite so. Do not disturb her, Mr. Brudenell: that will do very nicely. [*BRUDENELL nods also, and withdraws a little, watching her sympathetically. BURGOYNE resumes his former position, and takes out a handsome gold chronometer.*] Now then, are those preparations made? We must not detain Mr. Dudgeon.

By this time RICHARD'S hands are bound behind him; and the noose is round his neck. The two soldiers take the shaft of the wagon, ready to pull it away. The executioner, standing in the cart behind RICHARD, makes a sign to the SERGEANT.

SERGEANT [*to BURGOYNE*]. Ready, sir.

BURGOYNE. Have you anything more to say, Mr. Dudgeon? It wants two minutes of twelve still.

RICHARD. [*in the strong voice of a man who has conquered the bitterness of death*]. Your watch is two minutes slow by the town clock, which I can see from here, General. [*The town clock strikes the first stroke of twelve. Involuntarily the people flinch at the sound, and a subdued groan breaks from them.*] Amen! my life for the world's future!

ANDERSON. [*shouting as he rushes into the market place*]. Amen; and stop the execution. [*He bursts through the line of soldiers opposite BURGOYNE, and rushes, panting, to the gallows.*] I am Anthony Anderson, the man you want.

The crowd, intensely excited, listens with all its ears. JUDITH, half rising, stares at him; then lifts her hands like one whose dearest prayer has been granted.

SWINDON. Indeed. Then you are just in time to take your place on the gallows. Arrest him.

At a sign from the SERGEANT, two soldiers come forward to seize ANDERSON.

ANDERSON. [*thrusting a paper under SWINDON's nose*]. There's my safe-conduct, sir.

SWINDON. [*taken aback*]. Safe-conduct! Are you—!

ANDERSON. [*emphatically*]. I am. [*The two soldiers take him by the elbows.*] Tell these men to take their hands off me.

SWINDON. [*to the men*]. Let him go.

SERGEANT. Fall back.

The two men return to their places. The townsfolk raise a cheer; and begin to exchange exultant looks, with a presentiment of triumph as they see their Pastor speaking with their enemies in the gate.

ANDERSON. [*exhaling a deep breath of relief, and dabbing his perspiring brow with his handkerchief*]. Thank God, I was in time!

BURGOYNE. [*calm as ever, and still watch in hand*]. Ample time, sir. Plenty of time. I should never dream of hanging any gentleman by an American clock. [*He puts up his watch.*]

ANDERSON. Yes: we are some minutes ahead of you already, General. Now tell them to take the rope from the neck of that American citizen.

BURGOYNE. [*to the executioner in the cart—very politely*]. Kindly undo Mr. Dudgeon.

The executioner takes the rope from RICHARD'S neck, unties has hands, and helps him on with his coat.

JUDITH. [*stealing timidly to ANDERSON*]. Tony.

ANDERSON. [*putting his arm round her shoulders and bantering her affectionately*]. Well what do you think of you husband, *now*, eh?—eh??—eh???

JUDITH. I am ashamed—[*She hides her face against his breast.*]

BURGOYNE. [*to SWINDON*]. You look disappointed, Major Swindon.

SWINDON. You look defeated, General Burgoyne.

BURGOYNE. I am, sir; and I am humane enough to be glad of it. [*RICHARD jumps down from the cart, BRUDENELL offering his hand to help him, and runs to ANDERSON, whose left hand he shakes heartily, the right being occupied by JUDITH.*] By the way, Mr. Anderson, I do not quite understand. The safe-conduct was for a commander of the militia. I understand you are a—[*he looks as pointedly as his good manners permit at the riding boots, the pistols, and RICHARD's coat, and adds*] a clergyman.

ANDERSON. [*between JUDITH and RICHARD*]. Sir: it is in the hour of trial that a man finds his true profession. This foolish young man [*placing his hand on RICHARD'S shoulder*] boasted himself the Devil's Disciple; but when the hour of trial came to him, he found that it was his destiny to suffer and be faithful to the death. I thought myself a decent minister of the gospel of peace; but when the hour of trial came to me, I found that it was my destiny to be a man of action and that my place was amid the thunder of the captains and the shouting. So I am starting life at fifty as

Captain Anthony Anderson of the Springtown militia; and the Devil's Disciple here will start presently as the Reverend Richard Dudgeon, and wag his pow in my old pulpit, and give good advice to this silly sentimental little wife of mine [*putting his other hand on her shoulder. She steals a glance at RICHARD to see how the prospect pleases him*]. Your mother told me, Richard, that I should never have chosen Judith if I'd been born for the ministry. I am afraid she was right; so, by your leave, you may keep my coat and I'll keep yours.

RICHARD. Minister—I should say Captain. I have behaved like a fool.

JUDITH. Like a hero.

RICHARD. Much the same thing, perhaps. [*With some bitterness towards himself*] But no: if I had been any good, I should have done for you what you did for me, instead of making a vain sacrifice.

ANDERSON. Not vain, my boy. It takes all sorts to make a world—saints as well as soldiers. [*Turning to BURGOYNE*] And now, General, time presses; and America is in a hurry. Have you realized that though you may occupy towns and win battles, you cannot conquer a nation?

BURGOYNE. My good sir, without a Conquest you cannot have an aristocracy. Come and settle the matter at my quarters.

ANDERSON. At your service, sir. [*To RICHARD*] See Judith home for me, will you, my boy? [*He hands her over to him.*] Now General. [*He goes busily up the market place towards the Town Hall, Leaving JUDITH and RICHARD together. BURGOYNE follows him a step or two; then checks himself and turns to RICHARD.*]

BURGOYNE. Oh, by the way, Mr. Dudgeon, I shall be glad to see you at lunch at half-past one. [*He pauses a moment, and adds, with politely veiled slyness*] Bring Mrs. Anderson, if she will be so good. [*To SWINDON, who is fuming*] Take it quietly, Major Swindon: your friend the British soldier can stand up to anything except the British War Office. [*He follows ANDERSON.*]

SERGEANT [*to SWINDON*]. What orders, sir?

SWINDON. [*savagely*]. Orders! What use are orders now? There's no army. Back to quarters; and be d—[*He turns on his heel and goes.*]

SERGEANT [*pugnacious and patriotic, repudiating the idea of defeat*]. 'Tention. Now then: cock up your chins, and show 'em you don't care a damn for 'em. Slope arms! Fours! Wheel! Quick march!

The drum marks time with a tremendous bang; the band strikes up British Grenadiers; and the sergeant, BRUDENELL, and the English troops march off defiantly to their quarters. The townsfolk press in behind, and follow them up the market, jeering at them; and the town band, a very primitive affair, brings up the rear, playing Yankee Doodle. Essie, who comes in with them, runs to RICHARD.

ESSIE. Oh, Dick!

RICHARD. [*good-humoredly, but wilfully*]. Now, now: come, come! I don't mind being hanged; but I will not be cried over.

ESSIE. No, I promise. I'll be good. [*She tries to restrain her tears, but cannot.*] I—I want to see where the soldiers are going to. [*She goes a little way up the market, pretending to look after the crowd.*]

JUDITH. Promise me you will never tell him.

RICHARD. Don't be afraid.

They shake hands on it.

ESSIE. [*calling to them*]. They're coming back. They want you.

Jubilation in the market. The townsfolk surge back again in wild enthusiasm with their band, and hoist RICHARD on their shoulders, cheering him.

CURTAIN.

SHAW'S NOTES TO THE DEVIL'S DISCIPLE

BURGOYNE.

General John Burgoyne, who is presented in this play for the first time (as far as I am aware) on the English stage, is not a conventional stage soldier, but as faithful a portrait as it is in the nature of stage portraits to be. His objection to profane swearing is not borrowed from Mr. Gilbert's H. M. S. Pinafore: it is taken from the Code of Instructions drawn up by himself for his officers when he introduced Light Horse into the English army. His opinion that English soldiers should be treated as thinking beings was no doubt as unwelcome to the military authorities of his time, when nothing was thought of ordering a soldier a thousand lashes, as it will be to those modern victims of the flagellation neurosis who are so anxious to revive that discredited sport. His military reports are very clever as criticisms, and are humane and enlightened within certain aristocratic limits, best illustrated perhaps by his declaration, which now sounds so curious, that he should blush to ask for promotion on any other ground than that of family influence. As a parliamentary candidate, Burgoyne took our common expression "fighting an election" so very literally that he led his supporters to the poll at Preston in 1768 with a loaded pistol in each hand, and won the seat, though he was fined 1,000 pounds, and denounced by Junius, for the pistols.

It is only within quite recent years that any general recognition has become possible for the feeling that led Burgoyne, a professed enemy of oppression in India and elsewhere, to accept his American command when so many other officers threw up their commissions rather than serve in a civil war against the Colonies. His biographer De Fonblanque, writing in 1876, evidently regarded his position as indefensible. Nowadays, it is sufficient to say that Burgoyne was an Imperialist. He sympathized with the colonists; but when they proposed as a remedy the disruption of the Empire, he regarded that as a step backward in civilization. As he put it to the House of Commons, "while we remember that we are contending against brothers and fellow subjects, we must also remember that we are contending in this crisis for the fate of the British Empire." Eighty-four years after his defeat, his republican conquerors themselves engaged in a civil war for the integrity of their Union. In 1886 the Whigs who represented the anti-Burgoyne tradition of American Independence in English politics, abandoned Gladstone and made common cause with their political opponents in defence of the Union between England and Ireland. Only the other day England sent 200,000 men into the field south of the equator to fight out the question whether South Africa should develop as a Federation of British Colonies or as an independent Afrikander United States. In all these cases the Unionists who were detached from their parties were called renegades, as Burgoyne was. That, of course, is only one of the unfortunate consequences of the fact that mankind, being for the most part incapable of politics, accepts vituperation as an easy and congenial substitute. Whether Burgoyne or Washington, Lincoln or Davis, Gladstone or Bright, Mr. Chamberlain or Mr. Leonard Courtney was in the right will never be settled, because it will never be possible to prove that the government of the victor has been better for mankind than the government of the vanquished would have been. It is true that the victors have no doubt on the point; but to the dramatist, that certainty of theirs is only part of the human comedy. The American Unionist is often a Separatist as to Ireland; the English Unionist often sympathizes with the Polish Home Ruler; and both English and American Unionists are apt to be Disruptionists as regards that Imperial Ancient of Days, the Empire of China. Both are Unionists concerning Canada, but with a difference as to the precise application to it of the Monroe doctrine. As for me, the dramatist, I smile, and lead the conversation back to Burgoyne.

Burgoyne's surrender at Saratoga made him that occasionally necessary part of our British system, a scapegoat. The explanation of his defeat given in the play is founded on a passage quoted by De Fonblanque from Fitzmaurice's Life of Lord Shelburne, as follows: "Lord George Germain, having among other peculiarities a particular dislike to be put out of his way on any occasion, had arranged to call at his office on his way to the country to sign the dispatches; but as those addressed to Howe had not been faircopied, and he was not disposed to be balked of his projected visit to Kent, they were not signed then and were forgotten on his return home." These were the dispatches instructing Sir William Howe, who was in New York, to effect a junction at Albany with Burgoyne, who had marched from Boston for that purpose. Burgoyne got as far as Saratoga, where, failing the expected reinforcement, he was hopelessly outnumbered, and his officers picked off, Boer fashion, by the American farmer-sharpshooters. His own collar was pierced by a bullet. The publicity of his defeat, however, was more than compensated at home by the fact that Lord George's trip to Kent had not been interfered with, and that nobody knew about the oversight of the dispatch. The policy of the English Government and Court for the next two years was simply concealment of Germain's neglect. Burgoyne's demand for an inquiry was defeated in the House of Commons by the court party; and when he at last obtained a committee, the king got rid of it by a prorogation. When Burgoyne realized what had happened about the instructions to Howe [the scene in which I have represented him as learning it before Saratoga is not historical: the truth did not dawn on him until many months afterwards] the king actually took advantage of his being a prisoner of war in England on parole, and ordered him to return to America into captivity. Burgoyne immediately resigned all his appointments; and this practically closed his military career, though he was afterwards made Commander of the Forces in Ireland for the purpose of banishing him from parliament.

The episode illustrates the curious perversion of the English sense of honor when the privileges and prestige of the aristocracy are at stake. Mr. Frank Harris said, after the disastrous battle of Modder River, that the English, having lost America a century ago because they preferred George III, were quite prepared to lose South Africa to-day because they preferred aristocratic commanders to successful ones. Horace Walpole, when the parliamentary recess came at a critical period of the

War of Independence, said that the Lords could not be expected to lose their pheasant shooting for the sake of America. In the working class, which, like all classes, has its own official aristocracy, there is the same reluctance to discredit an institution or to "do a man out of his job." At bottom, of course, this apparently shameless sacrifice of great public interests to petty personal ones, is simply the preference of the ordinary man for the things he can feel and understand to the things that are beyond his capacity. It is stupidity, not dishonesty.

Burgoyne fell a victim to this stupidity in two ways. Not only was he thrown over, in spite of his high character and distinguished services, to screen a court favorite who had actually been cashiered for cowardice and misconduct in the field fifteen years before; but his peculiar critical temperament and talent, artistic, satirical, rather histrionic, and his fastidious delicacy of sentiment, his fine spirit and humanity, were just the qualities to make him disliked by stupid people because of their dread of ironic criticism. Long after his death, Thackeray, who had an intense sense of human character, but was typically stupid in valuing and interpreting it, instinctively sneered at him and exulted in his defeat. That sneer represents the common English attitude towards the Burgoyne type. Every instance in which the critical genius is defeated, and the stupid genius (for both temperaments have their genius) "muddles through all right," is popular in England. But Burgoyne's failure was not the work of his own temperament, but of the stupid temperament. What man could do under the circumstances he did, and did handsomely and loftily. He fell, and his ideal empire was dismembered, not through his own misconduct, but because Sir George Germain overestimated the importance of his Kentish holiday, and underestimated the difficulty of conquering those remote and inferior creatures, the colonists. And King George and the rest of the nation agreed, on the whole, with Germain. It is a significant point that in America, where Burgoyne was an enemy and an invader, he was admired and praised. The climate there is no doubt more favorable to intellectual vivacity.

I have described Burgoyne's temperament as rather histrionic; and the reader will have observed that the Burgoyne of the Devil's Disciple is a man who plays his part in life, and makes all its points, in the manner of a born high comedian. If he had been killed at Saratoga, with all his comedies unwritten, and his plan for turning As You Like It into a Beggar's Opera unconceived, I should still have painted the same picture of him on the strength of his reply to the articles of capitulation proposed to him by his American conqueror General Gates. Here they are:

PROPOSITION.

1. General Burgoyne's army being reduced by repeated defeats, by desertion, sickness, etc., their provisions exhausted, their military horses, tents and baggage taken or destroyed, their retreat cut off, and their camp invested, they can only be allowed to surrender as prisoners of war.

ANSWER.

1. Lieut.-General Burgoyne's army, however reduced, will never admit that their retreat is cut off while they have arms in their hands.

PROPOSITION.

2. The officers and soldiers may keep the baggage belonging to them. The generals of the United States never permit individuals to be pillaged.

ANSWER.

2. Noted.

PROPOSITION.

3. The troops under his Excellency General Burgoyne will be conducted by the most convenient route to New England, marching by easy marches, and sufficiently provided for by the way.

ANSWER.

3. Agreed.

PROPOSITION.

4. The officers will be admitted on parole and will be treated with the liberality customary in such cases, so long as they, by proper behaviour, continue to deserve it; but those who are apprehended having broke their parole, as some British officers have done, must expect to be close confined.

ANSWER.

4. There being no officer in this army, under, or capable of being under, the description of breaking parole, this article needs no answer.

PROPOSITION.

5. All public stores, artillery, arms, ammunition, carriages, horses, etc., etc., must be delivered to commissaries appointed to receive them.

ANSWER.

5. All public stores may be delivered, arms excepted.

PROPOSITION.

6. These terms being agreed to and signed, the troops under his Excellency's, General Burgoyne's command, may be drawn up in their encampments, where they will be ordered to ground their arms, and may thereupon be marched to the river-side on their way to Bennington.

ANSWER.

6. This article is inadmissible in any extremity. Sooner than this army will consent to ground their arms in their encampments, they will rush on the enemy determined to take no quarter.

And, later on, "If General Gates does not mean to recede from the 6th article, the treaty ends at once: the army will to a man proceed to any act of desperation sooner than submit to that article."

Here you have the man at his Burgoynest. Need I add that he had his own way; and that when the actual ceremony of surrender came, he would have played poor General Gates off the stage, had not that commander risen to the occasion by handing him back his sword.

In connection with the reference to Indians with scalping knives, who, with the troops hired from Germany, made up about half Burgoyne's force, I may mention that Burgoyne offered two of them a reward to guide a Miss McCrea, betrothed to one of the English officers, into the English lines.

The two braves quarrelled about the reward; and the more sensitive of them, as a protest against the unfairness of the other, tomahawked the young lady. The usual retaliations were proposed under the popular titles of justice and so forth; but as the tribe of the slayer would certainly have followed suit by a massacre of whites on the Canadian frontier, Burgoyne was compelled to forgive the crime, to the intense disgust of indignant Christendom.

BRUDENELL.

Brudenell is also a real person. At least an artillery chaplain of that name distinguished himself at Saratoga by reading the burial service over Major Fraser under fire, and by a quite readable adventure, chronicled by Burgoyne, with Lady Harriet Ackland. Lady Harriet's husband achieved the remarkable feat of killing himself, instead of his adversary, in a duel. He overbalanced himself in the heat of his swordsmanship, and fell with his head against a pebble. Lady Harriet then married the warrior chaplain, who, like Anthony Anderson in the play, seems to have mistaken his natural profession.

The rest of the Devil's Disciple may have actually occurred, like most stories invented by dramatists; but I cannot produce any documents. Major Swindon's name is invented; but the man, of course, is real. There are dozens of him extant to this day.

THE END